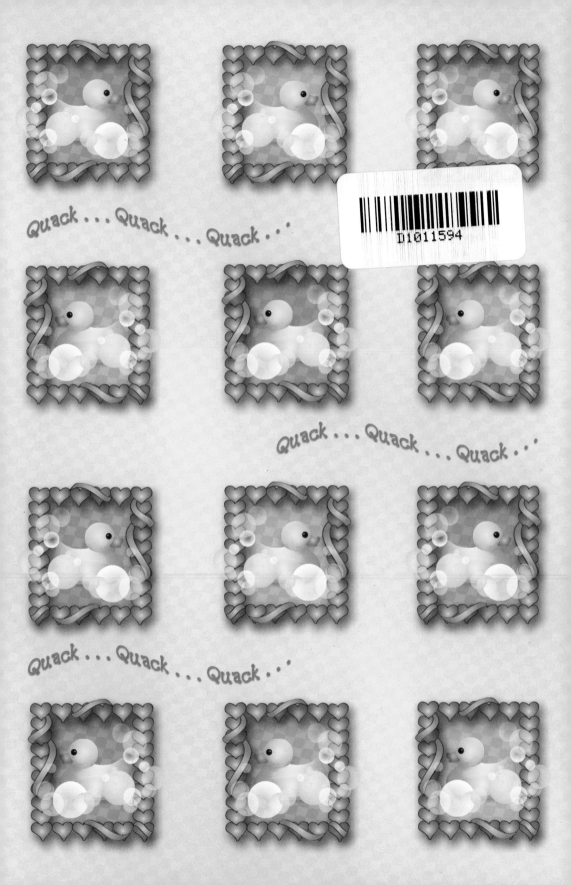

Quack . . . Quack . . . Quack . . .

Quack . . . Quack . . . Quack . . .

Quack . . . Quack . . . Quack . . .

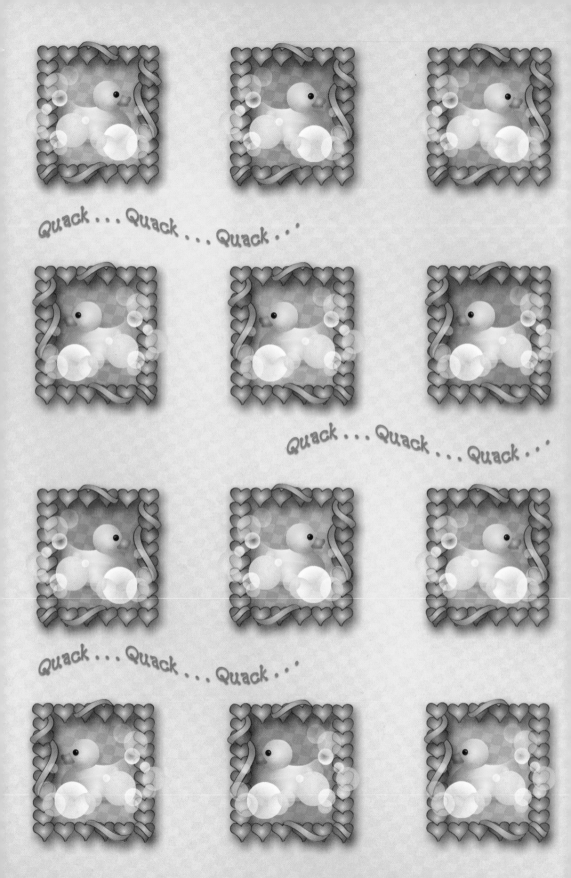

Quack . . . Quack . . . Quack . . .

Quack . . . Quack . . . Quack . . .

Quack . . . Quack . . . Quack . . .

JEANNE BICE

CREATOR OF THE QUACKER FACTORY

Presents

THE
RUBBER DUCK
PRINCIPLE

QUACK YOUR WAY TO HAPPY

with **LEE** and **TIM BICE**

Bice Library
Boca Raton, Florida

www.quackerfactory.com

Library of Congress Cataloging-in-Publication Data
is available through the Library of Congress.

© 2009 Jeanne Bice, Lee Bice and Tim Bice

ISBN-10: 0-615-31675-1
ISBN-13: 978-0-615-31675-8

Publisher: Bice Library
        160 W. Camino Real-295
        Boca Raton, FL 33432

Cover and interior design by Larissa Hise Henoch

Dedication

To Butchy—

Husband and Father. He taught us all how to march
to the tune of a different drummer.

Acknowledgments

"We Are Family!"

First of all I would like to thank my daughter, Lee and my son, Tim. Together we worked very hard on this project and it was a fun experience for our family. We spent hours in a back bedroom at my house telling stories of our lives, with Lee and Tim typing and typing and, of course, me talking and talking. At one point we just broke up and rolled with laughter and giggles when Lee said she felt like a computer program as she fixed all of our mistakes. We are so grateful that we have had this chance to share our journey with you.

I can't say enough about Larissa Henoch whose amazing creativity and graphic design made "The Principle" truly come to life. Thank you Larissa I love the way you've learned to "Quack."

READ THROUGH OR OPEN AT RANDOM ... FROM TIM

I would like to thank my good friend John Furr for spending hours and hours searching through boxes of hand written pages of my stream of consciousness babbling to find much of the material we used in this book and for his help with editing the final version.

To Heath Hansen whose creativity and support were key, many thanks.

We would like to thank all of the great people at Health Communications Inc. for years of loving support and encouragement. Especially Tom Sand for his expert guidance, Peter Vegso for always believing and Craig Jarvie for watching all the details.

Lastly, thanks to everyone at Quacker Factory—Richard Long, Kate Sheridan, Tiago Ramos, and Page Hammett; and of course our families and friends who all made special sacrifices so that we would have the time needed to put this whole thing together.

QUACK! QUACK!

Contents

Cherish Your Friends and Forgive Your Enemies

Happy's Gonna Happen Today (and Everyday!)

Take Time to Play

The Miracle of Happy

Finding Your Happy

What is HAPPY? And where can I find it? Like so many people I thought I'd find Happy in many places, or from many things, or from experiences. Mainly I believed that it took other people or things to create my happiness.

> "Oh, if I could just lose 50 pounds, I'd be Happy."
>
> "Oh, if I just found the right man to take care of me, I'd be Happy"
>
> "Oh, if I could just have that new car, I'd be Happy"
>
> "Oh, if I could just have a baby, I'd be Happy"
>
> "Oh, if I could just get that promotion, I'd be Happy"
>
> "Oh, if I earned more money, now I'd be Happy"
>
> "Oh, if I could live in New York/Hollywood/Paris/etc, I'd be Happy"

As I got older, fell in love and started a family, I came to realize Happy is not a destination. Happy isn't just about things you can buy. No, I came to discover that Happy comes from the choices we make and the way we think about our experiences on life's journey. The choices we make and the habits we develop can lead us closer and closer to fulfillment and joy.

As a young wife and mother I made great choices. My journey was on the road to a wonderful life filled with joy. I thought I had it all wrapped up in a big pink bow. Suddenly, with no warning, one day my husband died and "POOF" it was all gone. And my life changed forever.

For a long time I wondered if I would ever find Happy

Do what makes your heart sing

vi

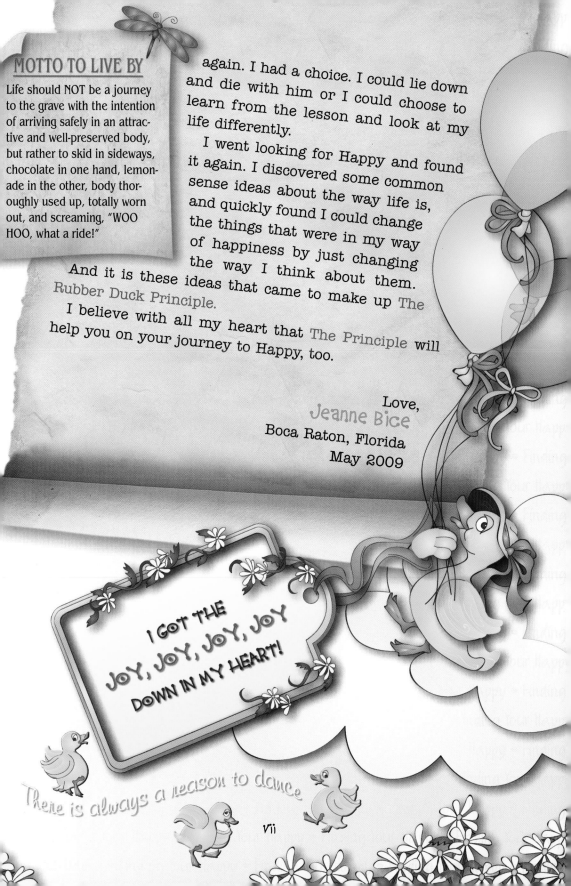

MOTTO TO LIVE BY

Life should NOT be a journey to the grave with the intention of arriving safely in an attractive and well-preserved body, but rather to skid in sideways, chocolate in one hand, lemonade in the other, body thoroughly used up, totally worn out, and screaming, "WOO HOO, what a ride!"

again. I had a choice. I could lie down and die with him or I could choose to learn from the lesson and look at my life differently.

I went looking for Happy and found it again. I discovered some common sense ideas about the way life is, and quickly found I could change the things that were in my way of happiness by just changing the way I think about them.

And it is these ideas that came to make up The Rubber Duck Principle.

I believe with all my heart that The Principle will help you on your journey to Happy, too.

Love,
Jeanne Bice
Boca Raton, Florida
May 2009

I GOT THE
JOY, JOY, JOY
DOWN IN MY HEART!

There is always a reason to dance

THE
RUBBER DUCK
PRINCIPLE

If you can't change something . . .

change the way you think about it!

QUACK YOUR WAY TO HAPPY

A Journey to Happy!

In order to begin a journey we must first decide if it is one that we want to take. I truly believe that God meant for us to live life happily. So let's admit to each other that life is at times less than Happy and commit to doing what we can to make a change.

The Rubber Duck Principle

For years both professionally and personally there have been things in my life that I couldn't change that have kept me from finding my Happy. I couldn't lose weight, I couldn't pay my bills, I had customer's who wouldn't accept my ideas or my products. The list goes on and on and we all have obstacles in our life that no matter how hard we try, we can't change. They get in the way of our Happy.

If you can't change something in your life, change the way you think about it. That's it. An idea so simple it seems like it couldn't be true. For many years I was a non-believer and pooh-poohed the idea.

My son and I started the Quacker Factory in 1991 and throughout the years when we have come up against obstacles in our business Tim always says, **"Mom if you can't change the way it is change the way you think about it."** And when I am as frustrated as I get when these situations present themselves I get pissed off. I have yelled at him, kicked him out of my office and told him that you can't just change your mind, you have to change the things that are wrong.

One time some years ago we had a buyer we were working with who would not see our vision and would not work with us and in fact wanted nothing to do with us. This was a new buyer hired by a long time and fairly large account that we did not want to lose. I started doing my usual ranting and raving about these things I clearly had no control over and wanted Tim to talk to her boss and get her fired. Or otherwise show how stupidly she was behaving. And in his usual fashion he said, **"Mom, if you can't change the way it is change the way you think about it."**

Boy, you wanna talk mad. I was absolutely livid. I couldn't understand why he was willing to just let this great account go and not get in there and fix it.

Once I got over my temper tantrum and calmed down, I began to think. I couldn't accept that we could fix the problem just by sitting around on our fat asses, but I also could see that Tim's thinking was right. The account had hired this person and they were going to back her up. So I began to really dig deep and look at how I was thinking about the problem at hand. Then I changed the way I was thinking about it.

Within the space of 6 weeks the buyer was off on a new and exciting opportunity for herself and the owner of the company who always understood our line was the one again buying it. The whole thing changed in the blink of an eye and we were back on track.

It was an amazing WOW! moment for me. I have since begun to look for more and more opportunities in life where I can change my thinking and make big changes in what happens in my life.

IT WAS AN AMAZING WOW! MOMENT FOR ME.

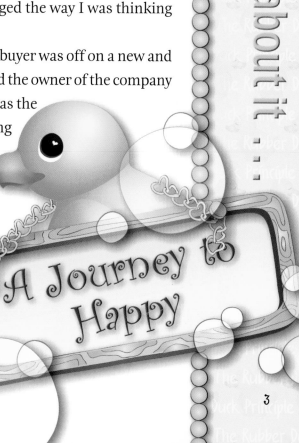

A Journey to Happy

The real magic in this discovery lies in the fact that the one and only thing we have any real control over in life is how we think about things.

I'm not saying that we don't need to make plans and go after the things we want in life. I'm not suggesting that we don't need to take action. We need to do all of those things to get what we want and to find our Happy. What I am saying is that when we come across something that gets in the way of getting what we want and finding our Happy and we see that no matter how hard we try we cannot change it, then it is time to change the way you look at it.

This idea does not only apply to dramatic and difficult situations, it works on every level and in every area of our lives if we only let it.

In the pages to come I would like to share some of the common sense ways I have used in my life which have been very helpful to me in changing my mind. And actually explore the reasons why something so seemingly simple and unbelievable can in truth be so powerful. So I invite you to join me in looking at all the fun and exciting ways of making change in our lives together.

THE REAL MAGIC IN THIS DISCOVERY LIES IN THE FACT THAT THE ONE AND ONLY THING WE HAVE ANY REAL CONTROL OVER IN LIFE IS HOW WE THINK ABOUT THINGS.

you can do it

4

The Rubber Duck Principle

To Change,
or Not to Change . . .

FACE
EACH NEW DAY
HAPPY!
ALL YOU HAVE TO
DO . . .
IS
DO IT!

Let me give you a for instance. Things we can't change, the boss, the in-laws, the time the mail comes. Things we can change, the coffee we drink, the doctor we see, what internet provider we use. Changing the things we can is the easy part. You don't like the coffee, the doctor, the internet provider, what do you do? Well you change them, of course. Now for the things we can't change. If we don't like our boss, can we just change jobs? Probably not and for very good reasons. But everyday you come home from work tired and crabby because you Hate the Boss. Here's where The Principle comes into play.

The only thing in life we have any control over is the way we think about things. We can't control how the boss treats us or how our spouse or children treat us. But we can control how we think about it. It is the only real power we have in life and we are always ready to give it away. We let our habits and knee jerk responses dictate how we react to and think about things. I say it's time to take that power back.

We can choose to get angry and hurt about the way the boss treats us or we can choose something more positive and upbeat and maybe even healthier for us to think about. If you break the old habits and do things differently, you will find that your perception of the situation is different and that your reality has changed.

Next thing you know, you find you are less troubled by your boss and if you're not careful they might even get nice on you. And all you did was to think about it a different way.

Too easy you say! Maybe not. Happy's a habit. Follow along with me and let's take a journey to Happy together.

A Truly Ducky Story

I was attending a seminar in Greensboro, North Carolina, for CEOs of companies from all over America. I was the oldest person there, and the only woman.

Now before you get the wrong impression, I must tell you that I was the CEO of an outdoor flea market booth in Delray Beach, Florida, selling embellished clothing that I designed and made by hand. (But, in fairness to myself, I should add it was a double booth!)

I'd been invited to this five-day seminar by my dear friends Lee and Suzannah Kleese. They thought I needed a vacation with loving friends. I thought I needed the love much more than the seminar. (Turned out I was wrong!)

For the first three days I sat there with these young men who all talked about their 5-year plans, their 10-year plans—so they could retire by the time they were 40. There I was a 55 year-old widow, selling clothes at a flea market! My only plan was to pay the bills and keep food on the table. But I did my best to join in.

> WE TALKED AND TALKED, WE **LAUGHED** AND . . .

We talked and talked, we laughed and cried. By the end of three days we had spilled our fears, our anger, our hurts—everything that was slowing down our progress and keeping us from reaching our highest potential.

On the fourth and fifth days we were told we all had to stay in the same hotel. But on the way there the van carrying us pulled into a Wal-Mart parking lot. We were given an instruction sheet explaining 'why' we were there:

splish splash

OUR MISSION: SHOP AS A CHILD. Buy things that a child would buy to make him Happy. Pleasurable things. Playful things. Silly things. We could buy whatever we wanted, but we HAD to buy two things: 1 rubber ducky and some bubble bath.

And the instruction sheet also said:

When you get back to the hotel tonight, you must:
• Fill the bath in your room with water and bubble bath
• Get in the bath
• Write about your experience

THE ONLY THING WE COULDN'T DO, WAS PUT THE BUBBLE BATH IN THE MAIN LOBBY FOUNTAIN . . .

Now this was not easy for me. You see I never really was a child. 'Silly' did not come easy to me. Fun was not on my agenda. And no matter how hard people dug, they were never going to cut through my very thick shell to get at my anger, my fear and my very hurt inner self! I had protected it very well, for too long.

But I was raised to be an obedient little girl, so I followed my instructions and did my homework. I bought some bubble blowing stuff, a paddle and ball, jacks and, of course, ONE RUBBER DUCK and bubble bath.

When we got back to the hotel, everyone piled into a large, beautiful suite. There they had pizza and other kid foods delivered to us, and we were given new instructions: We were to play like children, and then go back to our room and take our bubble bath. The only thing we couldn't do was put bubble bath in the main lobby fountain . . . apparently bubble bath powder breaks fountains, and the hotel was tired of replacing them.

Well, the playing began, and I just sat on a couch with two other men, who like me, could not believe what was happening before our eyes. There was finger paint on the ground, writing on the walls, the drapes were pulled down, the furniture

Love Those Bubbles

was tipped over . . . and silly string was just everywhere. Boys can be SO destructive.

The other two men and I watched the whole mess unfold, our mouths hanging open and judgment written all over our faces. Not one of us moved an inch from the couch, except to eat pizza. All my toys were still in the bag. In fact, the only thing I did want to do is shout, "Stop it! Pick up this mess and go to your rooms . . . you are all grounded for a week."

Eventually, we were all told it was time to go to our rooms and take our bath. OH, how I hate taking a bath. I wasn't going to do this either. I simply wasn't doing it. It wasn't like they were going to check me for wrinkled hands or toes in the morning.

> **Live your life,**
> **Love your bath tub.**

When I got back to my room I put on my PJs and started reading a book. Then 'the guilt' began to trickle in. I took a look at my ducky and felt even more guilty. Then I thought . . . maybe they could find out if I didn't take my bath. Just like I knew back in college that the nuns would find out if I had sex before I got married . . . they could smell it!

So reluctantly I filled the tub, poured in a capful of bubble bath, and tossed in my ducky, who happily landed tail side up. I, however, was a little more

THINK About Life DIFFERENTLY

careful about putting myself in . . . one toe at a time until the water felt just right. Now as I mentioned, I am not a bubble bather. To get in a tub and sit there and soak is not relaxing to me in the least and I felt very silly doing it with the duck. But being the good girl that I am I forged ahead with my assignment.

I was to play with childlike excitement so I gave it a shot and tossed the duck across the tub. He landed upside down but immediately popped upright and never lost that little ducky smile. I pushed him under, he popped back up. I splashed him, and it rolled right off his back (as one would expect it would). Before I knew it, jaded old me was having a very good time and I truly found myself giggling like a little school girl.

And as I sat there, giggling beneath a pile of bubbles, it hit me. This bath was a lot like life. If I were to take the time to try new things and think about life differently, I could quickly and easily change my experience of it. This duck was always smiling and no matter what came his way he

AND AS I SAT THERE, **GIGGLING** BENEATH A PILE OF BUBBLES, IT HIT ME . . .

LIFE

THINK Positive
. . . CHANGE
The Rubber Duck Principle

Must.Change.Attitude.

–Anonymous

always went with the flow, stayed upright and proved to be unsinkable.

On that evening in a bathtub at a small hotel in Greensboro, North Carolina I learned the lesson of the little rubber duck. Although it happened many years ago this experience was life changing for me. It truly got me thinking about the way I think about things. I hope that by sharing these thoughts you will begin to experience change in your thinking and that it will lead to positive change in your life too.

If you need a lift go get yourself some bubble bath and a little rubber duck and try it for yourself. I hope it is as fun and enlightening for you as it was for me.

Just What the World Needs

ell, can you look at a rubber duck and not smile? I don't think so. I challenge you to go find a rubber duck, look at it and see if you can keep from smiling. I keep myself surrounded by rubber ducks to always remind myself to laugh and to look at things differently.

A rubber duck knows its purpose in life.

"To make people Smile"—"To bring joy into one's life."

FOLLOW THE DUCK

A rubber duck is unsinkable. No matter what you do to him—tip him on his side—flip him upside down—hold him on the bottom of the tub . . . Bam, he springs right back to the surface and floats away; bringing smiles to everyone he meets along the way!

When we know our purpose and are in PERFECT HARMONY, we are Unsinkable!

UNSINKABLE . . .

WHY A RUBBER DUCK?

Life is Good!

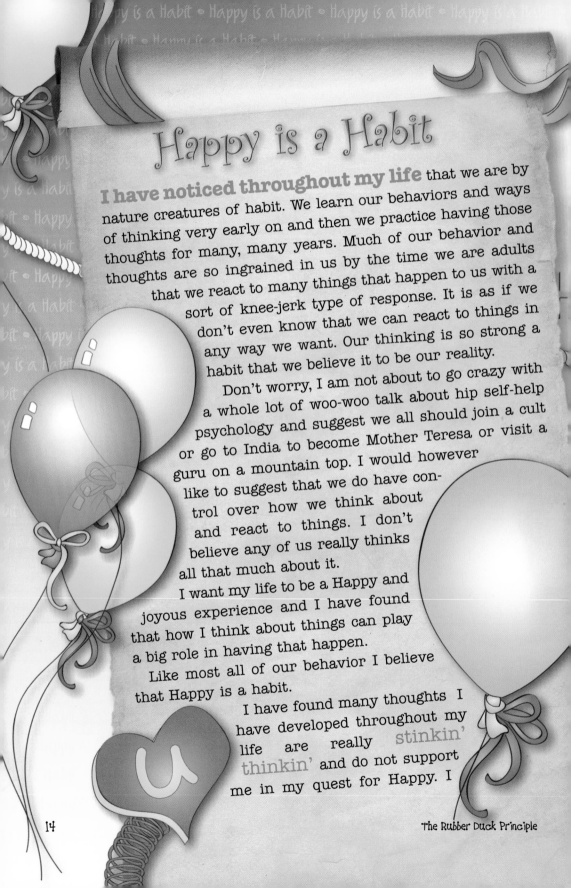

Happy is a Habit

I have noticed throughout my life that we are by nature creatures of habit. We learn our behaviors and ways of thinking very early on and then we practice having those thoughts for many, many years. Much of our behavior and thoughts are so ingrained in us by the time we are adults that we react to many things that happen to us with a sort of knee-jerk type of response. It is as if we don't even know that we can react to things in any way we want. Our thinking is so strong a habit that we believe it to be our reality.

Don't worry, I am not about to go crazy with a whole lot of woo-woo talk about hip self-help psychology and suggest we all should join a cult or go to India to become Mother Teresa or visit a guru on a mountain top. I would however like to suggest that we do have control over how we think about and react to things. I don't believe any of us really thinks all that much about it.

I want my life to be a Happy and joyous experience and I have found that how I think about things can play a big role in having that happen.

Like most all of our behavior I believe that Happy is a habit.

I have found many thoughts I have developed throughout my life are really *stinkin' thinkin'* and do not support me in my quest for Happy. I

The Rubber Duck Principle

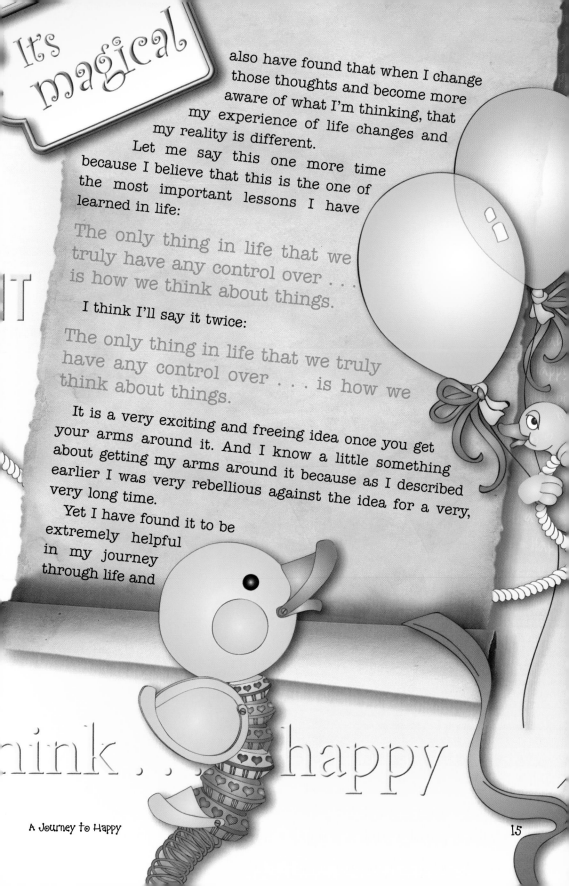

It's magical

also have found that when I change those thoughts and become more aware of what I'm thinking, that my experience of life changes and my reality is different.

Let me say this one more time because I believe that this is the one of the most important lessons I have learned in life:

The only thing in life that we truly have any control over . . . is how we think about things.

I think I'll say it twice:

The only thing in life that we truly have any control over . . . is how we think about things.

It is a very exciting and freeing idea once you get your arms around it. And I know a little something about getting my arms around it because as I described earlier I was very rebellious against the idea for a very, very long time.

Yet I have found it to be extremely helpful in my journey through life and

think . . . happy

in my never-ending pursuit of Happy. I have also found that it is easy to still get caught up in the old stinkin' thinkin' because I have had more than sixty some years of practicing it. Over the last couple of years of playing with the idea of changing my thinking I have discovered that there are some basic tools we can use that can help us to break the old habits and look at life differently so we can experience it differently.

As I have said many times in the past I am no expert I'm just a woman looking for her Happy. The ideas that I have assembled here are just good common sense and I have had the experience of change in my life by using them.

If you are a person who would like to have more Happy in your life I invite you to give them a try.

I have found at the beginning of the adventure that is changing your thinking, it is very helpful to take some time each day to sit down alone in a quiet spot and be introspective. Lay your head back, breathe deep, and relax.

believe

Start to truly examine the way you experience life and how you think about things.

What are the things in life that come between you and your Happy that you have not been able to change. It doesn't matter if they are big or small, start to look at how you can think about the situation differently. It will take some time and practice to change as we have all had many years of practicing the way we are. And at the same time I have found that change in this way can happen in the blink of an eye.

Our thoughts are very powerful and I invite you to take a look at experiencing that power on a journey to find your Happy.

The pages that follow contain many different ideas which I hope will inspire you to find the ability to change your ways of thinking. I like to think of it as a toolbox. Reach in and look for the tool you need right now to change something in your life. Read from beginning to end or open to any random page and find an inspiration that might work for you today.

Have fun, explore, and most of all get Happy.

Go ahead change your mind.
It's a woman's prerogative!!!

Just believe

Believe

Follow the Duck!

The Rubber Duck Principle

Listen to Your Heart!

Deep inside you is the answer to finding the Happy in life. All we need to do is to listen to it. Let's decide together to find out what life has in store for us.

Your Heart's Desire

What is your deepest dream? The dream you keep dreaming day after day, night after night? The dream you just can't stop dreaming. The dream you keep deep inside your heart, so deep you may not even tell your best friend?

Most of us live our lives everyday with the same expectations. We are going to wake up and follow some daily routine that we followed yesterday and the day before . . . and it's the same routine we expect to follow tomorrow and for the rest of our lives. I did it myself for the longest time.

It's time to change that. **TODAY IS THE DAY.** Lets take all the balls we've been juggling in our daily lives, toss them up in the air, and see where they land.

dream BIG

think big think up!

IF YOU CAN DREAM IT, YOU CAN DO IT!

Get a better sense of direction . . .

God planted Our Dreams . . . You Can Trust God Let Go Let God . . . Come on! Give Him the chance to bring this Dream to Life . . .

It's alwa

"I'm just ducky!"
Believe This . . .

The Rubber Duck Principle

Your Heart's Desire is inside you! It was sprinkled inside when God created you. Keep an open mind. And listen to that inner voice that says 'This is what I've been looking for!'

Your Heart's Desire can change over time. Life is a journey. Everyday we're learning something new about the world, and it's possibilities we never even dreamed of. Life's experiences lead us to our Heart's Desire.

YOUR Heart's Desire belongs to **YOU.** But it doesn't always 'bite you in the behind' and say 'here I am!' We have to look for it and listen for it.

Fill Yourself Up With
• Your Dreams . . .
• Your Passion . . .
• Your Belief

God Is With Us Through
Our Ups & Downs . . .
Thank Him on Both Ends . . .

good time to believe in miracles.

it is
insideYOU

R, NEVER
UP . . . TRY, TRY,
AGAIN!

Just
Listen

YOUR
HEART'S DESIRE
BELONGS TO
YOU!

Where the
Dream Began

WE HAVE A LOT OF GIVE UPS MORE THAN UPS . . .

Learn to trust your instincts. Listen to your heart. As long as you have opened yourself up to possibilities, your heart will know what is the right thing to do. Listen carefully, I promise that what you need to find your Happy is right inside of you. You just need to listen until you hear it. And you will hear it! You'll feel it! You'll know from the goose bumps!

Secondly, you have to remember that there is no ONE right answer. You may have been meant to do many things with your life. You may have many heart's desires. Love them all, live them all. Now is not the time to worry about how it will get done. Now is the time to dream them up as big as they possibly can be. It is the only way to begin to find your Happy.

God wants us to DREAM BIG because He's a big God who wants to do big things through us.

Shaping a
DREAM

Planting Seeds of Hope that Bring Dreams to Life

DREAM

You are SI

the Rubber Duck Principle

TODAY could be the day your DREAMS come TRUE

DREAM BIG!

You're about to feel lighter, breezier and so much more hopeful! And for good reason: Like all the growing things around you, the dreams you've planted are ready to blossom. All they need is a little optimism. Tend to them daily and watch them bloom!

I'M GOOD AT WHAT I DO
I'M GOOD . . . I'M VERY GOOD!

We Trust Everyone Else....
Doctors, Lawyers & Indian
Chiefs, Car Mechanics,
Electricians & TV Salespeople

Things are going to be better than all right. They're going to be great!

BIG

DREAM

er and stronger than you think you are.

Listen to Your Heart

WHERE YOU GO FROM HERE IS UP TO YOU.

From Imagination to Realization

We all have a purpose. Where is yours waiting to be found? What's the one thing you want more than anything else in the whole world?

What is "Your burning heart's desire"?

Many people say to me that they want to win the lottery. But, this is not their dream, this is a wish, and that's OK, if you are lucky enough to win. However, a very small percentage of people do. And, of those that do, only a small percentage of them hold on to it. Why? Because it is not their dream.

How do you find your dream? Pray! Go to a quiet place inside of you. This is hard for me "cuz" my head talks more than my mouth. Now, if you know me, I'm sure you find that hard to believe. But, it's true! I have a real chatterbox going on in my head all the time.

So, work on setting your mind to quiet. Maybe a little bubble bath will help. Go outside and lay on the back lawn all by yourself. Clear out all the people and the clutter. Give yourself this treat. Don't feel guilty! You deserve it!

What is it you want? What would you do if you knew you would never fail? Do you want a husband, a baby, a new house, financial security! Think hard. What's been burning in your belly since you were a little person? What did you daydream about? What did you play make-believe about?

YOU ARE AN ORIGINAL . . . THERE IS NO ONE ELSE LIKE YOU IN THIS WHOLE, WIDE WORLD.

Believe With Your Whole Heart That This Is Your D

The Closer You Get . . .

Life you want

The Rubber Duck Principle
Change Your Lif

Give Yourself Some Time to Grow into it . . .

BIG mission calls

r someone with an

ver bigger **HEART!**

WARNING: Don't You Talk
Yourself Out of Your Dreams

What is Your
Dream . . . Build It

Putting It
Together

Make every effort to be
gentle with yourself

. . . If you're happy
and look at life in the
best way you can,
even when there are
problems, think positively!

When you TAKE TIME to tend to yourself now.

MY HAPPINESS IS TIED TO
HOW I FEEL ABOUT MYSELF

Dreamland

The Dream
Team

The Possibilities
are Limitless

Sometimes When . . .

relaxation

> Only as high as you reach can you grow.
> Only as far as you seek can you go.
> Only as deep as you look can you see.
> Only as much as you dream can you be.
> —KAREN RAVN

DREAM

We Believe . . .
Believe in Me . . .
I Do . . . I Do . . .
I Do . . .

Grow Into It!

It Seems too
Big for Me

Listen to Your Heart

Grand Champion Daydreamer

I remember when I was a child growing up in Fond du Lac, Wisconsin, I was the grand champion daydreamer. Sometimes I would just lie in the middle of a big field that stretched on forever and dream and dream and dream. The land stretched so far, and the sky seemed endless . . . I could just lie there in the middle of it all and visit anyone, anytime or anyplace. While the other kids played games, I would dream about what I wanted my life to be like when I grew up. I remember my grandpa telling my dad about me, "Ernie, that gal sure is lazy." But my dad knew what a dream was, and he always replied, "She's a hard working girl, let her have her dreams. They will take her to glory some day." My dad was my first daydream believer. And that was when I learned how important daydream believers are in your life.

When I finally decided to go

To find your **Happy** you first have to **Dream!** It's easy for little kids to dream, but it gets harder as we grow up.

The Rubber Duck Principle

Giggle all the time.

*Wake Up Sleepy
Jeanne . . .
Oh What Can It
Mean . . .
To a Day Dream
Believer!
Cheer Up Sleepy
Jeanne . . .*
—JOHN STEWART

BECOME
A
DREAMER

to QVC with my Quacker Factory clothing line, I was scared to death. I wasn't afraid of going on live television, but of failing on live television. But then I walked into the room where hosts Kathy Levine and Dan Hughes were sitting; they looked at my product and listened to my story. Kathy turned to Dan and said, "We can make this woman's dreams come true, she's going to be a star." And he said, "No doubt about it, the QVC customer is going to love Jeanne." And they were right . . . my dreams did come true.

See what really good dream believers can do for you . . . even when you don't believe in yourself? And remember, it wasn't just QVC show hosts who were my dream believers here. My dad was my dream believer when I was a kid . . . and today my dream believers include my kids, my brother, my relatives, my friends, my co-workers, my quackers . . . and I keep looking for more everyday.

There are always people out there who can help you dream, and help you along when you need support. Whether you are doubting your ability, are caught in rough waters, or just need to quack about your dreams . . . having friends around to support you is one of the most important parts of starting to dream.

Follow y

Pick a good
Friend to
be your Dream
Believer ...

DREAM

BELIEVE!

The Rubber Duck Principle

it's ok to
ayDREAM

IG

eams

DREAM

Insert Your Picture Here!

DREAM . . .

er • Gran
Grand
on Dayd
Grand
ion Dayd
Grand
ion Dayd
Grand
ion Dayd
Grand
ion Dayd

BEWARE THE DREAM CRUSHERS:
Beware the naysayers, the dream crushers. They will stop at nothing to tell you it simply won't work. They will laugh at your wall of dreams and ideas and say something like, "yeah, yeah, whatever you say Jeanne." Steer clear of these cynics whenever possible and align yourself with like minded people.

think Positive.

what is your
bigDREAM?

heart's desire

What happens on the porch, stays on the porch.

listen to
yourHEART!

Life isn't about waiting for the storm to p

The Rubber Duck Principle

Dream BIG

K, OK, OK . . . How do I know what my big dream is . . . You say it's inside me . . . God put it there when I was born . . . How come I'm not aware of it. Maybe I didn't get a dream . . . Sure you did . . . Everyone of us got "dreams" "Hearts Desires" "Wishes"

You need quiet time . . . Time to listen to you talking to you time.

We get so busy, busy, busy . . . Stressed, stressed, stressed . . . Nobody listens to nobody . . .

Take time . . . me time . . . yes you do have the time—make time—just for you . . .

Love more, and all good things will be yours!

No Matter Where You Go . . . There You Are.

. . . about learning to dance in the rain.

dream

heart's desire

Delight yourself in the LORD, and He will give you the desires of your heart.
—Psalm 37:4

I Believe that our best days are ahead and that when we embrace God into our lives—He will take us places that we never dreamed possible.

The Rubber Duck Principle

Literally Put It On the Wall

H ere is a fun thing I still do everyday as I look toward new thoughts and goals. It doesn't matter if they are big career oriented goals or if it is something like getting a new dining room table, this is a great way to help change the way you think about them. Get a sticky pad with all different colors, and a bunch of colored markers to write with. Then think of things you would like to have happen in your life and write down phrases on the notes that summarize your desires. Make sure to write them down in the present tense as if they have already happened.

SUCCESS!

Thank you God . . . for my thin & healthy body. I love it!

"I am a singing sensation!"

"My catering business is growing!"

"Publishers want my novel now!"

"QVC Yes!!!"

(only if that's what you really want!)

I have the best job in the whole wide world!

Once you've got them written, put them all over the place. Put them on your bathroom mirror (the last thing you see at night, and the first thing in the morning.) Put them on your refrigerator, your computer screen, or your rear view mirror, put it on the end of your nose. My most favorite spot of all is around the edge of my TV screen (there's never a day that my TV is not on in my life!) Put them wherever you know you spend a lot of time. This way you can be constantly reminded of your new thoughts and make new habits that can bring about the changes and successes in your life.

gather new thoughts and goals everyday

I AM HAPPY . . . .

I love the new man in my life . . . thank you God!

God bless you and keep you in His love!

SOO VERY HAPPY . . .

what do YOU want to accomplish in your LIFE?

BELIEVE!

I CAN DO IT!!!

Thank you God. I have more money than I will ever spend!

Invite God in!

fear less, **HOPE** more; eat less, **CHEW** more; whine less, **BREATHE** more; talk less, **SAY** more:

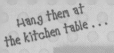

Put It On the Wall

My house is filled with signs. Tall ones, itsy-bitsy ones, all different colors and shapes . . . and they're on walls, in halls, embroidered on pillows and even hanging in the bathroom. You can't take a step and not see a sign somewhere. Expect a Miracle, Scatter Kindness, Believe . . . they're all over. But I don't just like having all those signs, I LOVE it.

I will say it has gotten to the point where my kids made me promise not to add any more signs. But I still sneak a few in now and then, when they're not looking. (Isn't it funny how it used to be the kids sneaking things by us, and now we have to sneak things past them?) If I find a sign I really like, I just have to have it.

After all, using signs has been very helpful to me in changing the way I think about things.

The most special sign

Years ago, while I was still putting my nose to the grindstone and getting nothing but a dirty nose, I had decided that I wanted nothing more than to sell my clothing on QVC. Well first I talked about doing it, and how great it would be . . . and then I whined about not doing it, and then I whined some more.

Finally, my son Tim got tired of all the negativity and said to me, "Mom, nothing else has seemed to work. I think it's

It's All Good

Live Simply
Love Generously
Speak Kindly
Care Deeply
Leave the rest to God

It's A Promise

Life is but a DREAM . . .

Hang them in your briefcase

Wish it Dream it Do it
Dream a Little Dream

Wish

JUST DO YOUR BEST

We Create Our Tomorrow's By What We Dream Today

The Rubber Duck Principle

Hang them in the garage

To have GROWN wise & KIND is the greatest SUCCESS of all

If mama ain't happy, ain't nobody happy

time to change the way we think about this. So why don't we make a great big sign that says 'QVC YES!!!' and put it on the wall."

So we made a great big sign out of a piece of tag board and hung it up on the wall of our office. Each day I would see the sign and become more and more positive about the opportunity that was out there and how good we would be on QVC.

God was taking care of me, because it wasn't long before I got a very special call from the Florida Department of Commerce. There was going to be an open audition for people to sell their products on QVC and—I couldn't believe it—but they wanted me to try out for it.

What I learned from this experience is that we are often very busy paddling our webbed feet to get out of the daily muck and mire in the water beneath us. What I think we need to do once in awhile is look up at the possibilities in the sky and all around us . . . and know that God will take care of the muck and mire if we just stop paddling so hard and stay focused on our dreams.

Twinkle Twinkle Little Star Do You Know How Loved You Are?

Be thankful ALWAYS

there is always, always, always something to be thankful for

live LIFE joyfully

Wish It

DO It

Fairy tale Wishes

Where Pigs Fly!

Happy

Just hang them!

There Cannot Be A CRISIS TODAY! My Schedule is Already FULL!

Think deeply, speak gently, love much, laugh a lot, work hard, give freely, trust God and be kind

GOOD FRIENDS ARE HARD TO FIND, HARDER TO LEAVE AND ... IMPOSSIBLE TO FORGET

the joy that you give to others is the joy that comes back to you

Make it a
great story!

We bring about what we persistently focus on. Stay focused on
what you want not what you don't. Intention—feel good today

Write it just
like you talk it . . .

Write . . . Write . . .
Write . . . Write . . . And
Write some
more . . .

Your Dream Book

ne thing I like to do to keep my Heart's Desire fresh in my mind is to keep a dream book. Dreams get one step closer to reality when we put them on paper. You can go out and get yourself a really nice notebook from the stationery store. But I think it can be more fun and personal to make one yourself. Decorate it with rhinestones, glitter or gold stars from a craft store. Make it as pretty as you can . . . and it will keep you inspired.

Use this notebook to write about your heart's desire. Write for pages and pages, talk up all the wonderful things your dream involves, from the little things you think are silly to the big things you know you want to do. This is YOUR heart's desire, and YOUR dream book, so DON'T HOLD BACK. Draw detailed pictures, stick figures and silly doodles related to your dream. Put stickers, stars and magazine clippings in it . . . whether they remind you of something, surprise you or inspire you. I'm always cutting stuff out and making collages to express my dreams and desires much in the same way I have done in the pages of this book. Make sure to have fun and keep it easy, this is meant to inspire not to add stress. Make believe you're a child again and really, really play.

Celebrate your successes, forgive your failures.
If you don't celebrate—the brain won't register it.

Dreams come a size too big so
we can grow into them.

Focus on all positive outcomes

Write 'til
your mind
can see it . . .

Just admit to yourself what you want, what you really want &
you increase the change of it occurring.

Don't just talk
about it . . . Write it . . . & Write more!

Write 'til your
mind believes it . . .

The Rubber Duck Principle
Write 'til the World believes you . . .
and you believe you . . .

Practice Thinking New Thoughts

I like to use signs and lists, like my Happy List, to always keep reinforcing my new thoughts. I also like to work these signs and lists into my prayers to continue to get used to my new ways of thinking.

For example:

Thank you God for more money than I could ever spend.

Thank you God for my fit and healthy body.

Thank you God for a great relationship with my boss.

I think you get the picture. Some people call these affirmations. I call them my new thinking exercises. I use them to practice my new thoughts just like a piano student uses the scales to learn to play. We can practice our new thoughts quickly and easily and have our experience of life change just like that.

People go into despair—or give up—the gap is too big from here to there. I really want it—how do I make it happen?

Create a new positive story about a future self. Now you've got a new story to live into. Write a letter from the thin Jeanne a year from now.

Take a moment to appreciate yourself to recognize how far you've come & what you've learned along the way. Behavior we celebrate grows even stronger.

Jeanne's Happy List

It's the time.
It's the place.
It Beckons . . .

Indoor plumbing

Television

My own
telephone

My car

French fries at
McDonald's

Dinner with
friends

Losing 10–50 pounds

No roots and a fresh haircut

Johnny Mathis Records

A phone call out of the blue from a friend

My bedroom at 4:00 p.m. everyday

A good card game

A trip to Office Depot

The trip to the dentist is over
for six months

The mailman put mail
at my front door

I have someone to take out the trash

I have a great nose and flat ears

I look wonderful in big sunglasses

Be
yourself.

You
can't please
everybody.
Don't let criticism
worry you.

The Rubber Duck Principle

Don't spend your time brooding over sorrows or mistakes

Don't take yourself too seriously. Don't think that somehow you should be protected from misfortune that befalls other people.

Keep busy at something

Do the things you enjoy doing.

A busy person never has time to be unhappy

Make up your mind to be happy. Learn to find pleasure in simple things.

Never borrow trouble.

Bubble thoughts
—Robert Lewis Stevenson

Make the best of your circumstances. No one has everything, and everyone has something

YOU CAN BE DUCKED AT ANY AGE . . .

Don't be one who never gets over things.

Bubble Bath

Since hate poisons the soul, do not cherish jealousy, avoid people who make you unhappy.

I can make people laugh

Caller ID

Surfing the internet, my mouse does the walking

An early Today's Special Value sell-out on QVC

The trick is to make the laughter outweigh the tears.

A plane trip on time—coming and going

My nails staying on in an important meeting

The color pink

Menopause—it sure made my life so much easier

Imaginary things are harder to bear than real ones

A good parade . . . love it

Playing jacks

Showing friends I can still blow smoke rings
even though I haven't smoked in 35 years

Lots of signs in my house

A new pair of shoes I don't have to break in

A really great faux diamond ring

My collections

Red carpet in my office

Someone lets me sneak into the other lane of traffic

The swimming pool is warm enough so that
I don't squeal when it hits my middle

Someone who enjoys my big mouth

My small rolling case that holds everything with ease,
including my heavy purse

A rerun of Matlock

Doo-wop music on PBS

Watching my favorite movie over and over again

My generator and no hurricanes so I never have to use it

I believe in magic, woo woo, and dreams

Gypsies on street corners

A singing, dancing duck

That kids get me . . . like with the videos on YouTube

The Rubber Duck Principle

Nothing to Fear!

Fear is the enemy to changing thoughts and running down the road to Happy. It's time to be ready to remove the fears and doubts that will defeat our journey.

Start Knowing Passion . . . Believe and Trust

hen it hurts to look back and you're scared to look ahead, look beside you—God is always there! When you're sure you're on the road to your heart's desire, don't get caught up in all those doubts and fears that your chatterbox keeps bringing up. You don't need to have all the answers. Just know what you want. Make sure you have it clear, have a passion about it. You can only take one step at a time. Most times these are baby steps. The biggest step is mustering up the courage to start. It's the job you never start that never gets done. Don't let the past hold you back. It's just the past. You're missing the good stuff.

Never Never Never Give Up

Being happy doesn't mean everything's perf

what are you MADE OF?

If you're going thru hell, keep going

G od didn't promise days without pain, laughter without sorrow, nor sun without rain, but He did promise strength for the day, comfort for the tears, and light for the way.
—Anonymous

Sometimes you have to go around a corner and back again to figure out where you are going!

do it **NOW** or forever **WISH** you had

What goes around **COMES** around.

" . . . the only thing we have to fear is fear itself "

SO FDR SAID . . .

...ns you decide to see beyond the imperfections.

Everything is bugging you . . .

Wouldn't It Be
Great . . . If You
Could Eat
What Bugs You!

EVER HAVE A DAY . . .
when everyone else
is having a Happy day . . .
But all you can think
of is I'm sinking
here guys . . .
HELP . . .
I'm sinking
I'm caught in the weeds . . .
Help . . . I'm going down
for the last time!
HELP!!!

Can't catch a deal
to save my soul . . .

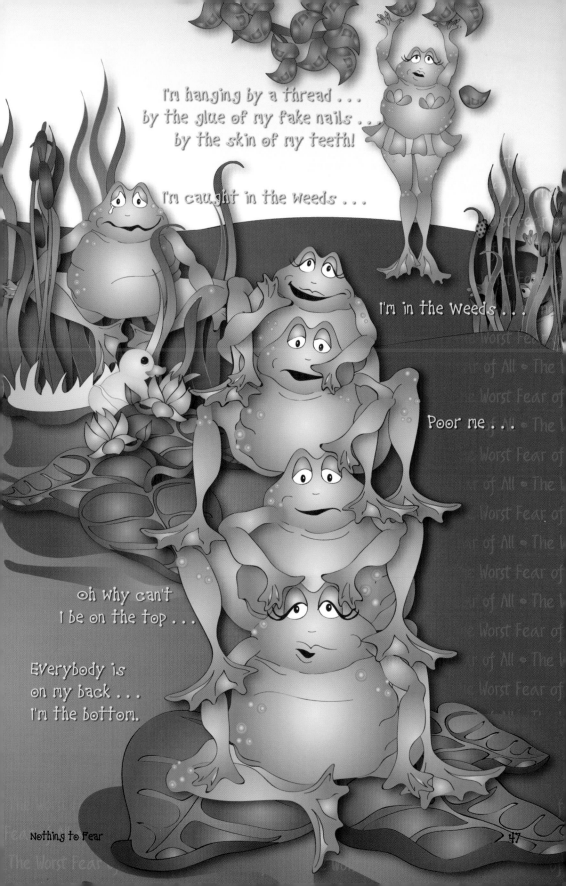

The Worst Fear of All

When my husband Butchie went to heaven, I was scared that I wouldn't be able to put my life back together again.

I was almost paralyzed with Fear. I'd had love, a wonderful home, stability, security, encouragement. Everything. And suddenly it was gone.

Oh, I had my wonderful children—one in college living in New York, another about to leave home. I had my parents and my dear brother. I had wonderful friends who cared and never forgot to call or invite me. But it wasn't the same. How could it ever be the same?

But the fear of loneliness wasn't the worst fear. The thing I feared the most was not knowing what to dream. For the first forty years of my life my dream had been to have a loving husband, a family, a Happy home. And I had it. What should I dream for now? I needed to make a living. I needed to work.

I took the advice of friends and sold the house in Wisconsin, and moved to Florida where my business partner and I had opened a second retail shop. Soon I started a clothing design and manufacturing business. For fifteen years I tried to work harder than anyone, work longer hours than anyone. I struggled to find someone who would save me and

"I felt like something was going to happen. I could feel the goose bumps forming."

DON'T CRY BECAUSE IT'S OVER SMILE BECAUSE IT HAPPENED

48

The Rubber Duck Principle

take care of me. All I got was very tired—hurt by all the wrong people—and broke.

At this point my son came back into my life—giving up his dream—and took over my business. At first, he worked it the same way I was doing it. Then one day he said, 'Mom, there's got to be a better way.'

I had spent thousands of dollars looking for answers. Taking seminars, buying tapes, watching videos and reading books. I had been on a personal quest, but just wasn't getting anywhere.

That's when I attended the workshop in North Carolina at the invitation of my friends, and took my first bubble bath with a rubber duck. It was then that I realized I could let go of some of my fear. I would be unsinkable. I had to learn to celebrate what I was and focus on what I do best. And let the water roll off my back. I had discovered The Rubber Duck Principle.

A Life Long Friend

I've known "Fear" all my life. Even as a kid in Wisconsin, I remember it being with me all the time—always pretending to be my 'friend'. Fear would pop up for silly things back then. I'd jump clear out of my skin every time I heard a siren of any kind. It did not matter if it was day or night, light or dark, morning, noon, or night – I would run in my closet and hide. Shaking as if the world were about to end. When I finally grew up some and got myself over that, I started worrying about looking too proud—a fear my dad put into me. "Don't get too big for your britches" was something I heard a million times.

Then there was my fear of roads that went any higher than a speed bump. Years later, when I was an adult, we went to Switzerland. I can say that I've toured the Alps by bus—I can't say I've seen any of them. I spent the entire bus trip under my coat singing Edelweiss to avoid the view as my bus twisted this way and that up the mountain roads (And no, the singing didn't help much. If you've heard me sing, you'd know why.)

Along with the fear of twisting, mountainous roads, is my stinkin' thinkin' that bridges are just not safe. Not any particular bridge. All bridges.

I remember one time Tim and I were driving to Florida from QVC in Pennsylvania . . . and as we were going through Charleston, South Carolina, we came to this tall, tall bridge. Ohhh, just thinking about it gives my tummy the ookies.

I'D JUMP CLEAR OUT OF MY SKIN EVERY TIME I HEARD A SIREN . . .

The Rubber Duck Principle

Thank goodness Tim was there; I would have turned right around and gone back to QVC if I'd been driving by myself.

But it got worse. As Tim and I were driving up the bridge, I realized construction workers had moved both lanes over to one side making them very skinny and very, very close to the edge. What was wrong that needed to be fixed? Was it safe to drive over? Were we going to die? I was sure of it!

MY STINKIN' THINKIN' THAT BRIDGES ARE JUST NOT SAFE . . .

Just as I was thinking all that, I heard Tim say, *"Oh my God, what are we going to do now?"* And suddenly, like a nightmare from my child-hood, coming from out of nowhere, there it was . . . the sound of a siren coming up behind us. That's right a siren! My two worst fears coming together at once, bringing me to an even higher level of anxiety. Fear was back at the worst possible moment. As it got closer we saw that it was an ambulance. How would it ever get past us? Tim decided the only thing we could do was to pull over into the right hand lane, which was, of course, on the very edge of the bridge. That scari-est bridge of all bridges ever, in all of bridge history . . . bridge. If only there was a *Sound of Music* song for that moment.

Let go . . . and let God.

Don't fear the future— God's already there.

"Don't Let Fear Sink You!"

FEAR WANTS TO BE YOUR 'FRIEND,' BUT BEWARE: IT'LL TAKE OVER YOUR LIFE IF YOU LET IT.

After forever and a lifetime, the ambulance finally

... SCARIEST BRIDGE OF ALL BRIDGES EVER, IN ALL OF BRIDGE HISTORY, BRIDGE.

passed us. We got back into our lane, and made our way off the bridge. We'd done it! Hip hip hooray! And that's when my eyes got as big as saucers. No, I wasn't Happy. There was another bridge just like the last one in front of us.

We made it over that bridge, though. And let me tell you, it taught me something about fear. There will always be another bridge to cross, another fear to face. *We're always going to be living with all kinds of fear in our life. To survive, we just have to puff up our rubber ducky with self-confidence and deal with them one at a time.*

A few years later I was back in South Carolina with my daughter, Lee, on a little road trip in the Low Country. We were visiting friends at the beach. One day we went for a drive, just the two of us. We stopped to buy baskets from women who sell them at roadside stands. We were having a ball. Suddenly

Believe

Release

Align

Expand

Keep Calm and Carry On

we're driving along and there it was again—'the dreaded Charleston Bridge'.

Lee asked if I wanted her to drive, but there was no place to pull off. I told her I could do it. Luckily there was little traffic. I told her not to talk to me, not to say anything. I asked her to keep the radio off and keep quiet! I drove right down the middle of the bridge. About a third of the way up, I begged her to talk to me. I was hyperventilating, breathing strange and begging her just to talk. Lee said, *"C'mon, Mom, you can do this. You're a big girl, just look straight ahead. Don't look sideways, don't look up, and don't look down, just look straight ahead."*

I heard myself praying fervently: *'Thank you, God, for my safeness . . . thank you, God, for my safeness.'* Over and over, that was my prayer. *'Thank you, God, for my safeness.'*

I did it. Now honestly I would choose never to go across the Charleston Bridge ever, ever, never, ever again! But I now know that if the time comes where I have to drive over it again, *'Thank you, God, for my safeness!' I will be safe.'*

Trust

Heal

Your LIFE is exactly what you THINK it is.

A Change for the Better

Exhale

Trust

fear . . . please . . . double DON'T!

RETHINK to where I want TO BE!

Tell Fear What You Think

There are so many ways to put fear in our lives . . . I will never get my dream . . . I want it all, but I don't think I'm good enough to get it . . . I'll never be thin enough . . . I'm not pretty enough . . . I'm not smart enough . . . I don't have the right materials . . . I don't know the right people . . . I don't have enough money . . . Only the kids at the "A" table win . . . I'm going to lose my job . . . My spouse won't let me . . . I can't do it alone . . . The world is going to hell in a hand basket. I could write a hundred, a thousand or a million more fears and I could still never cover them all.

But if you remember one thing, it should be this:

Your life is exactly what you think it is.

So you can choose your life to be one filled with fear. All you have to do is look to the other people who are swallowed up in their own worry and misery. Or you can choose your life to be filled with hope, possibility and probability. And you'll find all of that within yourself, even if it takes the help of a friend who shares your vision.

So look for the blessings, not the problems. Lets you and I find the courage to take fear on together. Ready? Read aloud with me, it's time to tell Fear just what we think.

"Fear, you're not our friend anymore,
and you can go to hell!"

> "Fear, you're not our friend anymore, and you can go to hell!"

> "Your life is exactly what you think it is."

Life is 10% What Happens to You AND 90% what you do WITH what happens to you.

—Anonymous

10 Things that Kill Success

1. I know what's going on
2. I have a foolproof plan
3. I don't need help
4. I don't have the smarts
5. I don't have the money
6. I don't have the time
7. I'm too old
8. I'm dreaming too big
9. I don't deserve it
10. Nobody understands what I want to do

The World is full of cactus, but you don't have to sit on it.

—WILL FOLEY

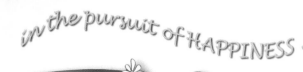

Every thought

that you think counts,
every positive thought
brings good things.
Every negative thought
pushes good away.

"Life Sucks"

What are you
going after with
this one?
It isn't that life sucks,
it's your
STINKIN' THINKIN'
that sucks!

Turn Tragic into MAGIC

About Change . . .

ne of the things I say all the time is "I Hate Change." "I just can't handle change." "Oh, I really agree, I hate change." Well, this is something we say without thinking. Yes, we like the comfort and ease of same, but think about this. You really DO WANT change . . .

YOU WANT THAT PROMOTION
THAT NEW HOUSE THAT NEW BABY
THAT NEW MAN
THAT HAPPY MARRIAGE
THAT BIGGER PAYCHECK
THAT NEW CAR
THAT GOLD MEDAL . . .
YOU DO WANT THAT CHANGE—

So why do we say "I Hate Change?" WE REALLY LOVE GOOD CHANGE. So, say it over and over and over again and now today, this very moment, you can choose to change the way your head thinks. As you think positive, you will have positive changes in every area of your life. IT'S MAGIC!

Just be careful. Make sure you know where you want to be when this ride is over, cuz you're gonna land somewhere new!

WOW!

LOVE, LOVE LOVE THAT GOOD CHANGE

change is GOOD . . . you go first

When Life Gives You Lemons

Life is filled with lemons . . . those lip puckering, lemons we all will have.

So, when the lemon truck pulls up to your life, you don't have to accept the delivery! Send it on its way . . . don't sign for things that aren't meant for you.

However, sometimes we think it's a lemon truck full of life-puckering problems when it may indeed be an event that produces a fruitful future for us. So, you need to really make a study of lemons—look at each lemon that comes into our lives. Are we going to let them destroy us, or will we let them help us become a "better me?"

Lemon "aid"

Do you see it as a tragedy or a blessing?

Life's Lemons

Lemons . . .
Good or bad—it's part of life's experiences and how we handle them shows the world how much pulp we have.

Seeds . . .
How you look at them is how you make it:
Lemon pie • Lemon "aid" • Margaritas • Decorate a tree
Everything in life does not need to be perfect to be perfect.
Each day comes bearing gifts. Untie the ribbons . . . maybe today it will be lemons, maybe it will be strawberries.

Lord . . . Help me to remember that nothing is going to happen to me today that you and I together can't handle.

Believe in Your Blessings

I believe that there is both good and evil in our lives. The good loves it when we are on the road to Happy. The evil can't stand it. Look for the blessings and angels we all have around us and the road is easy to see.

Take a Break!

Count Each Day a Blessing

With your imagination possibilities are endless. I think of how my life is blessed! A cure for stress and moving too fast is just to slow down. You're so busy doing for other's that you forget about you, your needs. Give yourself permission to take a break every now and then. Guilt free. Read a book, take a bubble bath, go for a walk. Make a joyful noise. Self-indulgence is good for the soul.

YOU ARE BLESSED

Read a good book!

The Rubber Duck Principle

Take a bubble bath . . .

SUCCESS is getting
what you **WANT.**
HAPPINESS is wanting
what you **GET!** —DALE CARNEGIE

Believe in Your Blessings

Go for a long walk . . .

THANK YOU!

THANK YOU!

I'm Sending You Many Thanks!

Thank You

thanks

There is always, always, always something to be thankful for

THANK youTHANKyou THANK youTHANKyou

THANK you!

THANK you!

THANK YOU!

The Rubber Duck Principle

Gratitude

I have discovered that one of the greatest ways to change my thinking is through being grateful.

You don't have to look for big things to be grateful for. When a stranger holds a door open, tell them, "Thank you" even if it makes you feel old. Or if a waiter does a great job for you, don't just assume a tip will let them know how you feel . . . say, "Thank you for the great service." Isn't it nice to know that you can make someone's day with just a few simple words.

Be grateful for everything that got you to where you are today. The most joyful and wonderful parts of your life. Remember that person who inspired you. What about the person who believed in you? The person who saw the sparkle in you, and made it shine brighter? Remember the days that went so well, and the moments that made you gladder than you've ever been? Be especially thankful for that. And if the positive people in your past are still around, seek them out and call or write a note to them. And even if they aren't, write a letter to them anyway, and put it in a book of memories . . . it will make you feel good now and whenever you want to look back on it.

Be grateful for everything you have right now. Appreciate the people around you every day. And be grateful for what you have. Sure there's the big stuff . . . your home, your job, your well-being. But also the small stuff . . . a

TO DO LIST:
- ☑ BE GRATEFUL
- ☑ THANK GOD
- ☑ COUNT YOUR BLESSINGS
- ☑ THANK FOR EVERYTHING

giggle you can't stop, an outfit that makes you look gorgeous, a movie that makes you cry because it's just that good.

Reflect upon your present blessings, of which every man has many—not on your past misfortunes, of which all men have some.

—CHARLES DICKENS

Be grateful for things that haven't even happened yet. God has a future plan for you, and if you are grateful for it and appreciate it, sight unseen it will be exactly the future that is the perfect one for you. Love the life you're going to get, and be grateful for it.

One of my favorite movie scenes ever is from Pretty Woman. Richard Gere is taking Julia Roberts to the opera . . . and while they are in an elevator, she turns to him and says something like . . .

"Thank you for the wonderful evening, in case I forget to tell you later."

That always gives me goose bumps. When's the last time you were grateful in advance of something happening?

Most importantly, be grateful for you! You make a bigger difference in your life than anyone, and there are lots of reasons to be grateful for you. If you are ever having any self-doubt or self-pity, here are some things you might want to tell yourself to help bring you back up:

"I am very grateful for me—I have many special talents and there isn't anybody else in the whole world I'd rather be."

"I love me just as I am. I am so grateful there is a me on this

The Rubber Duck Principle

earth and I absolutely deserve all the happiness I have."

"I am grateful to be alive and living this fairy tale of a life I have."

If you don't believe that it will make you feel happier to say these things, and to be grateful to yourself, well I can tell you that I'm living proof it works. Can you feel all the happiness that comes from me? That is because I am grateful for what is around me, but especially because I am grateful for me. Won't you come and be Happy with me? Just give it a try!

One morning I was writing one of my daily e-mails to people who help me with the business of the Quacker Factory. I headed the e-mail with my usual "Good morning!" and then I commented on how dismal the television newscasters were making our world, and that it was up to us to look for the sunshine and good things in life to keep ourselves Happy.

Later that day, I got an e-mail from my son, Tim. "Hey Mom, good heading today . . . did you mean to do it, or was it a typo?"

Well, I write "Good morning!" every day, so I didn't know what he was talking about. But I went back to look at the e-mail and I saw that I had written, "God morning!" No, I hadn't intended to do that, but I think God had a hand in it. It reminded me of what I think is the most important part of showing gratitude . . . we've got to be thankful to God everyday, because without Him, we wouldn't have anything. *When you're down to nothing, God is up to something.*

"We must find time to stop and thank the people who make a difference in our lives."

—ROBERT KENNEDY

CHANGE

HUG'S
ONE SIZE FITS ALL!
THANK YOU!

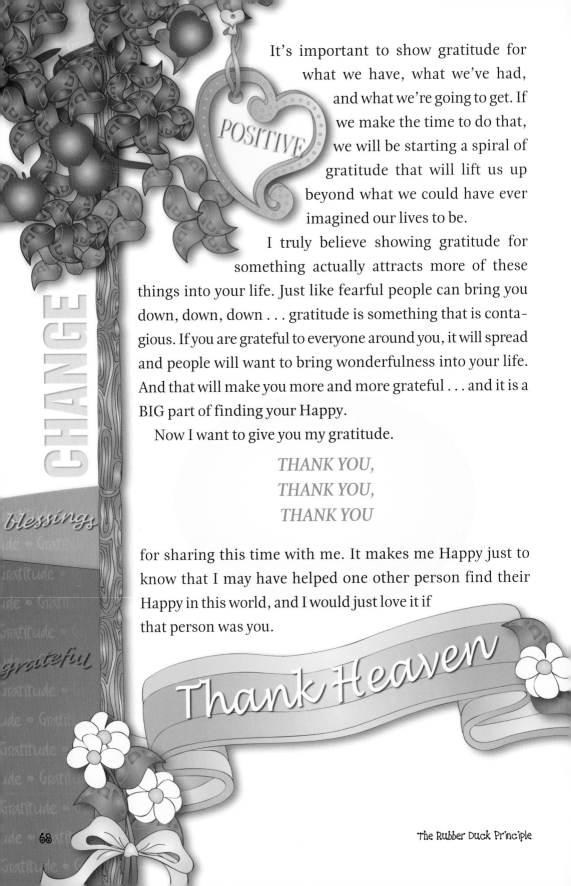

It's important to show gratitude for what we have, what we've had, and what we're going to get. If we make the time to do that, we will be starting a spiral of gratitude that will lift us up beyond what we could have ever imagined our lives to be.

I truly believe showing gratitude for something actually attracts more of these things into your life. Just like fearful people can bring you down, down, down . . . gratitude is something that is contagious. If you are grateful to everyone around you, it will spread and people will want to bring wonderfulness into your life. And that will make you more and more grateful . . . and it is a BIG part of finding your Happy.

Now I want to give you my gratitude.

THANK YOU,
THANK YOU,
THANK YOU

for sharing this time with me. It makes me Happy just to know that I may have helped one other person find their Happy in this world, and I would just love it if that person was you.

Perfect Harmony

Our stinkin' thinkin' not only causes us harm and takes us from our path it also hurts those around us. Let's be willing to make a change together for ourselves, and for those we love.

Talk-talk-talk
Chatter-chatter-chatter
Bitch-bitch-bitch

ow many times do you catch yourself tolerating something awful in your life and all you do is talk-talk-talk about it! Well, you aren't the only one. We all do it. I am a master at this. I bitch and kvetch for months and months until finally the voice in my head says *'Alright already, Jeanne, shit or get off the pot! I'm tired of hearing it, aren't you?'*

I've decided this process was the only way I could get over my guilt—and find the courage—to do what I had to do. It was my way of figuring out what was the right decision. God forbid I should make a mistake. I had to be perfect. It never occurred to me that my 'bitching' cancelled out perfect.

I have done this my whole life. *'Oh, poor me!'* This thing or that person was screwing up my perfect life. It was their fault—never mine. Then even I would get tired of listening to me. Finally I'd have to do something.

However, I have wasted months and months of being stuck till I do. And it slowed my rise to the top.

I know I am not alone. Substituting talk for action is perhaps the most common problem in the world today. Large companies spend time creating mission statements and strategies, but never actually put anything into action. Governments talk, talk, talk about solving problems but never get around to making the hard decisions.

This same thing goes on in our own lives. We plan, we

The Rubber Duck Principle

consider, we talk, and we 'bitch'. We take this as a sign of action. We think we're on the road to our dream, when what we really are doing is spinning our mouth! Motion is not movement.

I have found that all the bitching is just a habit I use to keep myself involved in stinkin' thinkin' and not make any real progress in changing my life. Listen to your thoughts, if you find that you are kvetching about something—that is probably a something about which you might want to change the way you're thinking.

Don't Believe Everything You Think

creating the LIFE you want

Chubby, Healthy and Happy!

Life was a piece of cake—A big cookie and peanut butter sandwich to me 'til I was 5 years old. I lived on Bell Street in Fond du Lac, WI. The neighborhood was full of kids. It was a short little street and we seemed to know everyone. The family across the street had a daughter, babysitter age, so she was mine. So I was in and out of their house all day long.

Everyone on the street were friends. I would pedal my bike up and down the street and was rewarded with food everywhere I went. My favorite was a peanut butter sandwich. Some days I had two or three between meals. I just loved, love, love food. It was a great reward for me, I knew I was loved when they gave me food.

My parents were a little older when they got married, 25 and 30. So most of my folk's friends had kids older. So I was a treat. I always felt like I was the princess of Bell Street. I loved it.

Then one day my folks announced they had bought their first house and we were moving to 5th Street. My parents were so excited. They were buying a home AND they were having another BABY. This was the first time I can remember feeling, I didn't like change, because I had the perfect life. Why would anyone want to leave this? Bell Street was a Heaven on Earth place for me. Well hang on . . . when my Dad said we're moving, we moved. No one had a vote and I was 4 1/2 years old. Why would I care? Well I did and it made me sad.

Spread Sunshine

The Rubber Duck Principle

you've got everything you need inside

But luckily they gave me food to cheer me up. The only really great thing about living on 5th Street was that my Dad's Aunt Lena and Uncle Joe lived two houses down the street. My Aunt Lena was as wide as she was tall and had been a nanny for many years before marrying Uncle Joe. She was a nurturer. She loved little children and had the need to be loved. My mom was always gone golfing, bridge, bowling, coffee with the girls, which meant I had a baby sitter a lot. Her name was Esse. She was from a very big family. She really didn't want to play with a kid so I was left to do whatever I wanted. In those days you could wander anywhere in the neighborhood as long as you didn't cross a street. One of my favorite places to go was Aunt Lena's—she always greeted you with homemade eggnog, saying it "builds healthy strong bodies and puts a little chubby in those cheeks." And another was a small neighborhood grocery around the corner filled with popsicles, ice cream bars and orange slices. OK—I can live with this. Just fill up the tank with goodies, you can handle anything. Food became my best friend.

Then one day, my new baby brother came home. We were exactly five years apart almost to the day. In fact he came home from the hospital on my fifth birthday, July 20th, 1944. And he became my responsibility. I was 5-years-old, but I became his mother. I wanted to make sure he had all the love in the world and he was a crying, sickly kid.

I never forgot how friends of my moms would come over and say, "Oh Mora, you should have left this one at the hospital. He's ugly and

THERE IS ONLY ONE YOU.

always sick and my God all he does is cry. Now look at Jeanne Marie, she is so chubby, healthy, and Happy. He is so skinny. If he would just stop crying long enough to eat something, maybe he would look better."

This made me love him all the more. I seemed to be the only one that did. I would put him in the buggy and push him around the block for hours just to keep him Happy. This was a big responsibility for a 5-year-old. I became an adult at age 5 and believe me, no one asked me to do this. This is what went on in my head. I took this on all by myself.

With this added responsibility in my life, food became my best friend. As long as I could eat, I remained Happy.

5th Street had lots of kids my age. We played house and school every day. It was great. I was always the mother or the teacher. At 7 or 8, I was making it my main purpose to convert all my friends to be Catholic. I always had a cause. I think I was always an old soul—more adult than child. I don't ever remember having a childhood after we left Bell Street.

When I was 9-years-old, we moved to Ledgeview Avenue. It was the prettiest house in the whole world. This was about the age that my baby fat became a problem to my Mom, and was the first time the doctor and she started talking diet to me. So now I had to start sneaking food and sneaking money from my folks to buy my all-time favorite popsicles or ice cream bars. Yes, this neighborhood also had a tiny grocery around the corner and one block away was Moses Super Market. The first of its kind. Now, the problem with sneaking food is

Do what you love, and you'll love what you do.

BE PROUD OF WHO YOU ARE!

that you never really have time to enjoy the food. You have to eat on the run. So, it killed part of the joy of food. It just made me sneak more—looking for the comfort feeling I wanted from it. On top of it, most of my friends were skinny and could eat anything!

My Mom worked full time so we ate out a lot. Hamburgers and french fries were a staple of our life and when my mom did cook, it was wonderful but, very German and heavy, I loved every moment of it. Lots of potatoes and bread and gravies. To this day, gravy bread is one of my favorite treats or juice bread.

By now, Dick and I were on our own a lot and I took up cooking. My parents entertained a lot, so I learned how to be Mother's little helper. I was her Sous Chef and cleaner upper. This way, I got to be the taster at the beginning and the eater of leftovers at the end. I was the Good Child . . .but I did get great rewards . . . wonderful Food.

Around the age of 12 or 13, my Dad announced we were moving to a farm. World War III broke out! My mom was not going and I was not going. Well she got a Buick and her first dishwasher & I got a horse. So, yes, we could be bought off and we moved to 4th Street Road. Dick and I never did get the hang of the horse. He was scared of it and I threw up the first and only time I rode it.

By the time we got to the farm I was the chief cook & bottle washer. I loved doing it. It gave me a reason to eat. I learned to cook tapioca pudding. I learned to make chili. All the heavy satisfying comfort foods. By now I was on a constant diet and I had all this stuff in my head about how I relate to food.

So as you can see at a very young age I learned how to think about food. And I have been practicing thinking about it for my whole life since. All of the diets I have failed at and all of the ones I have succeeded at (and then put all the weight back on) have helped me

love YOU!

to reinforce my stinkin' thinkin' about and towards food.

This is the one area of my life where I have not been able to, or have not wanted to, change my thinking. I have been able to change the way I think about money, I've changed the way I think about business, I've changed the way I think about relationships and even success itself. But I haven't arrived at real change in my thinking about food and fitness.

I am still troubled by thoughts of guilt, fear and humiliation. Even though I completely understand that these thoughts are of my own choosing and even though I know I can change the way I think about it, I still struggle in this one area.

So you see I completely understand the struggles that we put ourselves through because we are all human and we have learned from experience what our realities are. Yet every day I wake up I am filled with the belief and excitement that I will change the way I think about even this, the most challenging hurdle of my life.

I commit to you that I will continue to challenge myself to change my thinking and I invite you to join me in changing yours as we continue this glorious journey down the road to Happy. Just you, me, and our good friend the mighty Rubber Duck.

One of a KIND

LET THE WATER ROLL OFF YOUR BACK!

The Rubber Duck Principle
Recognize your potential

I Am Enough

It's safe to feel my feelings
I am enough—I do enough
Now I can relax and be myself
Thank you God, I'm a success
Now I can relax and enjoy myself
Since I'm already a success I can relax and enjoy myself.

I deserve to enjoy my life and success
I ask for what I want and accept it with joy and pleasure
I am enough and I deserve it
I love me—I like me
I am willing to let go of the past and forgive me
for screwing up so often
Thank you, God—I am safe and secure
I am enough!

I am willing to rescue my dream
I am letting go the need to make myself wrong
I am enough!
I am clear about my preferences
I am constantly moving toward my goal
I am enough!

Oh Happy Day!

Go Girl.

Never underestimate the value of the little moment

xoxo

surpass your dreams

I am very special, I am wonderful

I am the Best.

Perfect Harmony

77

A Goal is Attained One Step at a Time

There is no sudden leap to greatness
Your success lies in doing, day by day
Your upward reach comes from working well and carefully.

Good work done little by little becomes great work
Your house of success is built brick by brick.

A bottle fills drop by drop.
Adopt the pace of nature.
The secret is
patience.

GOOD WORK

I LOVE THE ME I AM TODAY,
THERE IS NO ONE ELSE LIKE ME.
I AM VERY SPECIAL,
I AM WONDERFUL,
I AM THE BEST!
I BELIEVE I AM THE BEST
THAT I CAN BE RIGHT NOW.

Every choice you make in life . . . the friends you choose to treasure, the clothes you choose to wear, the music you choose to listen to, the way you express your vision for yourself at home . . . everything you decide can make it easier to find your HAPPY.

. . . the biggest choice you have to make is to decide that you really LOVE yourself. You have to decide to BELIEVE that you deserve to find YOUR HAPPY. If you decide to do these things, you'll discover that everything you need is already INSIDE YOU.

Be proud of who you are.

78

You are enough just the way you are.

Love yourself. Be proud of who you are.

Stop blaming yourself for everything that goes wrong in the whole wide world . . .

In your own life, accept what's happened learn from the experience, forgive yourself, make plans to move on and then move on. Time will pass. Living well is the best life.

When there is nothing left but God, that is when you find out that God is all you need. Take 60 seconds and give this a shot! All you do is simply say the following small prayer:

Father, God bless me in
whatever it is that you know
I'll be needing this day!
And, may my life be full of your peace,
prosperity and power as I seek to have
a closer relationship with you.

When you want to talk about your dreams, imagine having someone on your side who will be there to give you all the reasons why you can have what you want. That's what friends are for.

LOOK WITHIN YOUR HEART

"YES" THERE WAS STUFF LAST YEAR THAT YOU WERENT HAPPY ABOUT.

OK, IT'S OVER. TAKE TIME TO FORGIVE YOURSELF AND MOVE ON.

Perfect Harmony

Love yourself.

Be in Perfect Harmony

"I'm strong to the finish cuz I eats my spinach. It's all I can stands . . . I can't stands no more." —Popeye the Sailor Man

What can't you stands no more in your life . . .

We need to "Believe" Just Believe . . . Believe all things are possible. Yet . . .

Progress is impossible without change. Change your Thinking . . . Change your life . . . Then you're unsinkable!

Dramatic life changes happen—Boom! In a moment. We can't always change a person or our situation. What we can change is our mind and the way we think, how we handle challenges, disappointments, and surprises that come our way day by day. You CAN change your life by just changing the way you think.

WE NEED TO BELIEVE JUST BELIEVE . . .

1. **Keep your nose out of other people's business.** You have enough to keep you busy running your own life.

2. **Avoid that knee jerk reaction thing.** Don't worry what others are thinking or saying about you. When you react to stuff like that, you just fill up your tank with anxiety and second guessing. Just watch what comes out of your mouth.

3. **Kindness Matters.** Give up your judgments. We don't want to hurt each other with our judgmental words. Scatter kindness each day. Keeps the wrinkles down.

4. **Let pissy go.** Kindness will just flow out of you. Everything happens for a reason and nothing happens by chance. Always look at the lesson in the experience. Be grateful for the stuff that comes into your life.

5. **Do no Harm.** Always ask yourself—Is it True? Is it kind? Is it necessary? Before speaking–avoid gossip. Try to be a Happy, helpful, kind person.

The Rubber Duck Principle

6. Control Freak? Ooops . . . let go the need to be in control. It's downright liberating. Life is so much sweeter . . . let someone else run the show.

7. Discover what your own life's lessons mean. Everyone has a story to tell and we can learn from them. Our own lessons are so much more important. Think about your lessons. What is God teaching us through them?

8. I'm right. I'm always right, and, I'm right all the time! The time spent arguing who is right could be better used being peaceful rather than right. Let go of need to be right.

9. Change your mind from agitated to peaceful. Change your mind from argumentative to kind.

10. Forgive yourself. Let the past go. Today is the day. Every day is a fresh start. Guilt-proof your life by forgiving yourself first. Never let yesterday fill up today and don't ruin today by worrying about tomorrow.

11. Choose your thoughts wisely. Surround yourself with love and peace. Happy songs, movies, funny friends.

12. Put yourself first. Only then can you be of help to others—through your example. Unless you are in harmony there is no way you can be any good to anyone including yourself.

Life is 10% What Happens to You AND 90% what you do WITH it. Be GREAT at this.

—*Anonymous*

Live Happy

Unforgettable

Perfect Harmony

Happy Day

81

The Law of the Garbage Truck

Many people are like garbage trucks. They run around full of garbage, full of frustration, full of anger, and full of disappointment. As their garbage piles up, they need a place to dump it and sometimes they'll dump it on you. Don't take it personally. Just smile, wave, wish them well, and move on. Don't take their garbage and spread it to other people at work, at home, or on the streets.

The bottom line is that successful people do not let garbage trucks takeover their day. Life's too short to wake up in the morning with regrets, so . . .

Love the people who treat you right and Pray for the ones who don't.

So I am wishing you a garbage-free day.

. . . SMILE, WAVE, WISH THEM WELL, AND MOVE ON!

JOY

you can't change yesterday, but you can ruin today, worrying about tomorrow

Live a more balanced, joyful life!

"Don't let yesterday fill up today!"

The Rubber Duck Principle

Fairy Tales Do Come True

We all have our Happy ending right inside of us. Let's leave behind the thoughts of what we didn't do or what we're not capable of and go find what it is we are.

Bibbity Bobbity Boo

We all believe in odd stuff . . .

We believe in Santa Claus, Easter Bunny
and the Tooth Fairy . . .

We believe April Showers bring May flowers . . .

March comes in like a lamb out like a lion . . .

Starve a cold, feed a fever . . .

The Sun will come out tomorrow . . .

Friday the 13th is bad luck along with walking
under a ladder and black cats crossing our path . . .

So, why can't we believe Fairy tales do come true?

So, as far as I'm concerned, we can all use a fairy godmother at any age, any stage of life. It's so reassuring to believe there is a special being who's there just for you.

Have you lost hope in the world you live in and feel the only one who has visited you is the screw-up fairy? Are you finding life has lost all of its sparkle and shine and you've forgotten how to let your imagination run free? Then you really are having trouble believing the Universe is full of goodies just for your picking. You have become a "curmudgeon" or the screw-up fairy has taken over your mind. It's time to let the magic back into your life.

Believing in magic is really, really important to create your perfect life. Magic helps us remember we live in a world of great gifts where everything is possible! It also makes it more fun and a heck of a lot more interesting.

We live through childhood by believing in magic, and wishes do come true. We make wishes on falling stars, on blown out birthday candles and butts of white horses. We know if we make a wish as we blow out the candles and don't tell anyone our wish, it will come true.

Life is a witch then you fly

We believe there is always someone who will save the day, from superman or woman to our guardian angel. Little girls grow up believing in Fairy Godmothers who have magical powers and they show up when we really need them. It's their job to rescue us— help us out of scary situations and help us to transform our lives from bad to wonderful and she says we will live happily ever after. When we grow up, we lose that magic feeling, that magic touch.

We become grown-ups. We turn into our mothers, but we always hold onto that secret fantasy, that secret hope and wish to have a fairy godmother. Tucked away in our hearts is the belief there is always someone wise and wonderful who can step in and save the day with a twinkle of the nose, a wave of their magical wand, or a dose of fairy dust. This is often why we think we need a man to run our lives and fix everything.

Whether she turns a pumpkin into a coach, helps you land the prince or a great job, shows you how beautiful you truly

It's never too late to live happily ever after!

are, protects you from wickedness or makes sure you live happily ever after . . . we all love to hope that she will someday show up and help us make life magical. We can learn how to harness the childhood technology for making dreams come true when we acknowledge that we can create our own magic in life.

When you're ready to remember the magic of being a girl, she helps us conjure the faith and optimism of childhood and connects us to all the mystical and magnificent possibilities of the universe. Like the beloved grandmother or aunt with special powers, she helps us believe in the magical divine powers of the universe and within ourselves. She represents our innocent, magical selves and the benevolent hand that reaches out to assist us in living our dreams.

Our Fairy Godmothers are wonderful, magical, mystical beings who show up in fairy tales in the nick of time, wand in hand, and help the heroine turn her dreams into reality and live life happily ever after.

Invite her into your life. Continue to believe in her and she will stay alive in your heart forever. Put fairy tale inspiration all around you. Read yourself fairy tales, put stuff on the walls.

Tack up words and sayings. Select passages that speak to things you want to magnetize into your life, such as the prince and new wardrobe you've been after.

Buy a wand. A wand is a magical tool of choice for all conjurers and witches—in fairy tales,

> Opportunities will present themselves to you. Things that hadn't come to you before will suddenly show up. You'll be in the "flow" of life.

and real life. In fairy tales, a wand represents magical powers and abilities. You can purchase a beautiful handmade wand with fancy trimmings and stones on the end, or buy a simple children's wand and keep it in a place you can see it. It is the emblem of magic in your mind; just owning one will make you feel more magical!

Keep fairy dust around. It's a symbol of magic and possibility that helps us remember life can be invented and created from nothing, and dreams can come true. It gives us hope. It also reminds us to focus our attention on making magic happen. Use gold or silver sparkles, pretty confetti, or buy some packaged fairy dust from Good Fairy Enterprises.

Be inspired by magical movies and TV shows. If you have children in your life, you already own a few magical videos. If not, rent or purchase your favorites—the ones you enjoyed as a child as well as newer releases. Any form of media that helps you tune into magical memories and uplifting feelings is perfect whenever you need a pick me up. Here are a few favorites: Peter Pan, Cinderella, Sleeping Beauty, Aladdin, The Little Mermaid and Splash. Also, very helpful in awakening the imagination and making you smile; Reruns of Bewitched and I Dream of Jeannie. Listen to your Fairy Godmother's advice.

Take personal responsibility. While it would be nice to clean up our messes and issues with one wave of the wand, even in fairy tales we are asked to

If you could ask your Fairy Godmother for three wishes, what would they be?

Awaken Wonder!

Magic Is What You Make It

BELIEVE in the MAGIC

Do you believe in miracles?

Wish Upon a Star

do our part in transforming our own lives. Before she waves a wand and snaps her fingers, our Fairy Godmother makes sure we get a life lesson unlike any other. It is the journey of becoming more of who we are meant to be that really leads us to the potential for happily ever after. It is only after we take the journey, with all the scary twists and bumps and dark characters that we are ready to take a leap of faith which leads us to the ultimate healing that changes our lives. So when you find yourself on one of those bumpy paths, don't ever give up hope . . . remember, it is all a process.

Appreciate her special support. She connects us to the goddess within by helping us believe in ourselves. The magical accessories are just to help us fake it until we make it. The true gift is the boost of confidence. While it may seem that Cinderella's life changed with just a twist of her wand, in truth, her fairy Godmother represents a true mother figure, a soul friend, who reached out a hand to help her onto the next rung of her life journey. By showing her some of life's options, she expanded Cinderella's ability to go after the greater things in life.

Ask for big presents, but accept whatever is given. The modern Cinderella might prefer a magical credit card with unlimited prepaid credit and a limo driver to take her shopping—and that's fine. But if you ask for a Visa Gold and a driver, and first get a Macy's gift certificate and cab fare . . . accept it gratefully. The Fairy Godmother sometimes tests us

Your Word is Your Wand. When you speak from your heart and say the words your soul has only dared whispered that's when miracles happen.

before she delivers the goods. Our grace and gratitude in the face of disappointment helps us remain humble and grounded when the big windfall occurs.

Get home by Midnight. The Fairy Godmother is also the voice inside our heads that guides us. She knows exactly when the magic of any given situation will wear off, and when to come home. Heed her guidance because it is always for your own good!

Wish upon a star every night. Or, write a wish a night on a small piece of paper and slip it under your pillow before you go to sleep. Your Fairy Godmother and the cosmic crew are always listening.

I **LOVE** it! It's what I've always wanted!

Kids Believe in Magic

As you begin to take time for yourself, remember that you are born a magical being. Once upon a time we all believed in magic. We believed in the magic of Christmas, the Tooth Fairy, the magician who performed at the circus, the magic of Super Man and Wonder Woman in the movies. We watched in wonder. We believed.

And we believed just as much in ourselves. We could do anything. We could be anything. We dreamed and we believed.

Just because you may have lost some of the magic along the way does not mean it is gone forever. You may have forgotten the magic, but it's not gone. It's simply hidden deep down in your heart.

The first thing you have to do is be **willing to believe** in the magic again. Believe, believe, believe that it is there inside of you. Believe that you can get to it again, and believe that it can completely change your life. There is just an unlimited world of possibilities out there, and all it takes is your little bit of magic to be open to them all.

The next part of finding your magic, and the biggest most importantest part of all, is to create an **"I Believe in Magic Day"** . . . a day dedicated to you, a day that you absolutely don't share with anyone but you. It's a day when you

Be Your Own Fairy Godmother!

Rubber Duck Principle

have to give your-self permission to play all day long. And you have to give yourself per-mission to become enchanted with life again.

I know, it may seem like a whole heck of a lot to ask other people to have them take responsibility for them-selves for one day . . . but consider all they've asked you to take on for them, and even all the clutter you've asked yourself to take on in your life. So what is one day where you and only you mat-ter? I'll tell you what it's good for . . . it is a small step on the path to getting what we deserve in life. And I hope you will take this one step with me, so that we can return to the magical life we deserve together.

Life isn't about waiting for the storm to pass. It's about learning to dance in the rain.

But what do we do with an entire day for ourselves? We can play, plan and reconnect with who we are, and what we are meant to be. On page 92 is my list of what you can do to make your **"I Believe in Magic Day"** a success.

Once you have given yourself one **"I Believe in Magic Day"** take it one step further. Make every day **"I Believe in Magic Day."** No, this doesn't mean you have to quit your job, neglect your family and ignore your friends. But it does mean that you should keep looking for what you want every day, and make sure you are giving your-self enough time in a day to live the life God wants you to live.

Believe What's in Your Head

So what are the beliefs that live in your head?
I'll share mine—you write yours. Mine are . . .
I'm a fat person, healthy, but fat.
I have a sore knee, never gets better.
I never have trouble sleeping.
I'm always scared. I have bad teeth.
I have ugly feet. I'm a great cook.
I love people and people love me.
I can't do that alone, I need a partner.
I don't deserve it. I'm not good enough.

Guess which ones are true?

All of them because I believe them!

What's in Your Head?

_____
_____
_____
_____
_____
_____
_____
_____
_____
_____
_____
_____

"We all have many gifts . . . find yours!"

Rubber Duck Principle

If Pigs Can Fly...
I Can Believe...

Believe
Believe Believe
in the Beauty of
Your Dreams

Life is sooo good!

"When you reach for the stars
you may not get one,
but you won't come up with a
handful of mud either."

Think Happy

I think we must have 60,000 thoughts going through our heads every single day . . . and if you're with me on any particular day, you know this isn't far off! (And, if you'll listen, I'll tell you about 50,000 of the ones that are going through my head right now.)

The point is, we all do a lot of thinking. How many of those thoughts that you have in a day would you say are about the people, places and things that make you Happy? 30%? 40%? 50%?

Happy thoughts do not just come by a Happy accident. They are a result of the way you decide to think, and the things you fill your life with everyday. If you think that you're a dumb person, then you will be a dumb person. If you think you're a procrastinator, then you will certainly procrastinate. If you think you're not capable of achieving your goals and finding your Happy, you never will.

You have to decide to be Happy, and to be a happy person. Choose to be Happy today, tomorrow and for the rest of your life. Because Happy is a habit.

Rubber Duck Principle

Happy is a Habit!

Keep Talkin' Happy Talk!

"Our HAPPINESS depends on the habit of the mind we cultivate. So practice happy thinking every day. Cultivate the merry heart, develop the happiness habit, and life will become a continual feast."
—Norman Vincent Peale

All seasons are beautiful for the person who carries happiness within!

Smile

HAPPY DAY!

cheer

C'mon Get Happy!

There is more inside you than you dare think....

Believe the Best is Yet to Be

Fairy Tales Do Come True

If you BELIEVE in YOURSELF …

When we can no longer change a situation . . . that's when we are challenged to **change** our thoughts.

I AM UNSINKABLE.

I didn't come here to lose.

WINNING *moment*

never give up … this may be your **miracle moment!** all things are **possible** …

Fly high

Go Team!

WIN!

SUCCESS!

BELIEVE IN YOURSELF …

HAPPINESS

We all wish you happiness … we are here to support yo

...soar! • Give them a little lift and watch their ... soar! • Give them a little lift and w...

...them a little lift a... their spirits soa... Give them a...

a little lift and w...

o will others!

Reach for your dreams and they will reach...

CHANGE!

believe in your dreams!

I BELIEVE YOU ARE BLESSED!

I BELIEVE IN YOU...

I WILL ALWAYS REMEMBER YOU...YOU ARE VERY SPECIAL

YOU CAN DO IT!!!

Give them a Little Lift and Watch their Spirits Soar!

The reason most people never reach their goals is they don't know what they want. Define your dreams . . . your heart's desire.

Believe they are believable and achievable . . . if you're having trouble doing this . . . find friends who believe in you.

Let them believe for you—'til you find the courage . . . they can help you fly above the clouds . . . above the storms you just have to let them help . . .

Believe in them . . . they believe in you!

Friends are kind to each other's hopes . . . they cherish each other's dreams . . .

I made it . . . half because I was willing to take a risk along the way . . . and half because there were lots of people who cared enough to help me . . . to believe in me!

Go Team!

We all have many gifts . . . find yours!

nd your passion!

Sound Track of Your Life

May today there be peace within. May you trust that you are exactly where you are meant to be. May you not forget the infinite possibilities that are born of faith in yourself and others. May you use the gifts that you have received, and pass on the love that has been given to you. May you be content with yourself just the way you are. Let this knowledge settle into your bones, and allow your soul the freedom to sing, dance, praise and love. It is there for each and every one of us.

DAY DREAM

DON'T SETTLE ... REACH HIGHER

Believe...

This Little Light of Mine. I'm Gonna Let it shine!

feel great about yourself regardless of the situation?

learn how to create a great mindset for yourself at any time—be it work or at home?

enjoy your work regardless of the stresses around you?

Don't get caught up in the how of things. If you're clear on what you want to change and why you want to change it, the how will come. Many significant things have been left undone because someone let the problem solving interfere with the decision-making.

If someone believes in you ... and you believe in you ... anything can happen. Your dreams can come true and live happily ever after

Rubber Duck Principle

"A year from now you may wish you had started today."

THE DREAM OF A LIFETIME

Life is "gonna" change no matter what . . . might as well enjoy it . . .

I am in the World to change the World.

I DARE YOU TO BELIEVE . . . THAT ALL THINGS ARE POSSIBLE!

LIVE YOUR LIFE WHILE YOU HAVE IT . . .
BE PROUD OF WHO YOU ARE . . .
LOVE YOU!
ONLY THEN CAN YOU CHANGE
THINGS IN YOUR LIFE . . .

Spend some time each day to daydream

Reach For the Stars...

Take personal responsibility. Never think that "it's not my job" It's a cop-out to say, "What can I do, I'm only one person." You don't need everyone's cooperation or anyone's permission to make changes. Remember this little gem, "If it's to be, it's up to me."

FOLLOWING YOUR DREAMS SHOWS OTHERS THAT IT IS POSSIBLE FOR THEIR DREAMS TO COME TRUE. I DARE YOU!

EACH DAY BELIEVE YOU ARE THE TYPE OF PERSON
WITH WHOM YOU WOULD LIKE TO BE BEST FRIENDS . . .
BELIEVE IN YOUR DREAMS
BELIEVE YOU MAKE A DIFFERENCE IN THIS WORLD
BELIEVE THERE IS ALWAYS A LIGHT AT THE END OF THE TUNNEL
BELIEVE THE BEST IS YET TO BE
BELIEVE IN YOURSELF . . .

Fairy Tales Do Come True

BELIEVE in YOURSELF

Opportunities are never lost; someone will take the ones you miss.

All achievement, all earned riches, have their beginning in an idea!

Don't wait for things to be right in order to begin. Change is messy. Things will never be just right. Follow Teddy Roosevelt's timeless advice, "Do what you can, with what you have, where you are."

"Thoughts are things," and powerful things at that, when they are mixed with definiteness of purpose, persistence, and a burning desire for their translation into riches, or other material objects.

JUST DARE TO BELIEVE ... CHANGE IS GREAT!

"Do one thing every day that scares you."
—Eleanor Roosevelt

"In any moment of decision the best thing you can do is the right thing, the next best thing is the wrong thing, and the worst thing you can do is nothing."
—Theodore Roosevelt

CHANCE

It's what YOU THINK that counts. You must have a DESIRE, you must have set up in your mind a DEFINITE MAJOR PURPOSE and you must stand by this purpose until it becomes an all-consuming obsession!

SIMPLE ACTS OF COURAGE LEAD TO GREAT ACTS OF COURAGE.

Let the voice that is telling you to take your turn speak louder. Listen to it and act. Take one step, even a small step, in the direction of your dreams.

The greatest danger for most of us is not that our aim is too high and we miss it, but that it is too low and we reach it.
—Michelangelo

Try something that you've been afraid to do and see where it takes you. You may be surprised to discover just how brave you are.

"When it comes to the future there are three kinds of people: Those who let it happen, those who make it happen and those who wonder what happened"

Rubber Duck Principle

Mirror, Mirror on the Wall

Let's take a look at ourselves knowing that we have nothing to fear. By looking at what we are and what we do that keep us from finding our Happy, it becomes simple to identify thoughts that we would like to change.

Mirror, Mirror on the Wall

I grew up in a home where the bathroom mirror was like our audience, our friend, someone to talk to.

The mirror helped my dad achieve great success in life. He had gotten a teaching degree from the University of Wisconsin, but after six months of teaching he realized it was not his dream job. So he went to work for the Carnation Milk Company. However that job entailed moving around the country. When my mom got pregnant in Iowa, he decided he needed to find a job where his family would have stability: same school, same church, same friends and relatives around all the time. My dad was the oldest of eight kids, so family was very important to him. He moved on to a job with the Department of Agriculture in Fond du Lac, Wisconsin, and this became their home for the rest of their lives.

My dad always had a dream—for as long as I can remember. His dream was to retire at 50 years of age with money to live a great life, and to have a second home in Florida, and a third home on Lake Winnebago.

To accomplish this, he'd say to my mom, 'We need to start our own business. The only way to make the money is to have your own business. A government job isn't going to get us there.'

Plus he really wanted to be his own boss. He was a great leader of people and he loved to sell. Remember this is a man who put himself through college making and selling bath tub beer during Prohibition!

One day he came home and announced he had figured it out. On his job he worked with farmers in the area and had grown to love going to farm auctions on Saturdays and Sundays. He thought he would make a great auctioneer. He could sell Real Estate while he learned the auction business. He would practice, and practice. He spent hours 'Crying' a make believe auction in the car. This is where he spent most of his days.

He would go to different auctioneers' auctions on the weekend to learn by observing their styles. Then during the week he'd teach himself the craft of "Crying an Auction," copying their styles.

In the morning while he was getting ready for work, and then again at night, he would practice in front of the bathroom mirror. He would greet the crowd. Chat about the farmer, and make it personal- He always felt a manure spreader would bring more money if they thought of it as 'John and Mary's manure spreader.' He would then start selling, and play with the crowd. *All these people lived in our bathroom mirror.*

Then at the end of his practice sessions he'd look himself straight in the eye and tell himself what was good and what needed work.

During the day he would work on those changes. In his car he sold to the steering wheel.

As long as he worked, he did this every day. He kept improving his craft this way. He coached himself into being one of the top auctioneers in the country.

> I GREW UP IN A HOME WHERE THE BATHROOM MIRROR WAS LIKE OUR AUDIENCE, OUR FRIEND, SOMEONE TO TALK TO.

What Do You Say to Your Mirror?

The mirror is a great tool to see yourself in action. Go ahead and try it! When you look in the mirror, what do you see? Are you afraid to look? Stand in front of the mirror and talk to it like it's your best friend. And talk out loud! While you're doing this, listen to what the voices in your head are saying back to you.

"Boy do you look fat." "My teeth are yellow." "Look at those wrinkles around my eyes."

Notice how you feel having a relationship with yourself.

"Oh, yeah! I love what I see!"

"You're old and fat and never going to be any different!"

"Look at those birthing hips!"

"You're never going to be a kid again!"

Who do you see looking back on you? Do you like what you see? Do you smile when you talk? Do you look people in the eye when you talk to them? What do you say to others? Is it interesting? Does it bring people joy when they listen to you?

It's an interesting experience, isn't it? It's good to do, because it's a way of beginning to know what you think and believe about yourself. I hope you like what you find in the mirror, many of us don't.

A great place for us to begin to change our thinking on this journey to Happy is to change the way we think about ourselves. If you look in the mirror and have negative thoughts, think of something about you that is positive and fun. It might be hard at first but it is something that gets easier with practice.

Sort of the same way my dad was not a great auctioneer the first time he tried to look at himself in the mirror and sell something, but with time and practice he became confident and changed to thinking that he was one of the best auctioneers in the country and that is what he became.

You can do the same with how you think about yourself. Give it a try and have some fun.

"You're never going to be a kid again!"

"You're old and fat and never going to be any different"

"My teeth are yellow."

"Boy do you look bat."

"Look at those birthing hips!"

SMILE

LOOK THEM IN THE EYE

BE INTERESTING

BRING JOY

"Oh, yeah! I love what I see!"

Mirror, Mirror on the Wall

I Wish You Enough . . .

I wish you enough sun
to keep your attitude bright

I wish you enough rain
to appreciate the sun more

I wish you enough happiness
to keep your spirit alive

I wish you enough pain
so that the smallest joys in life appear much bigger

I wish you enough gain
to satisfy your wanting

I wish you enough loss
to appreciate all that you possess

I wish you enough Hello's
to get you through the
Final Goodbye.

Love everything abo

Pick you for a friend . . . pick you first!

Count yourself as a blessing

Make friends with yourself . . .

Enjoy yourself . . .

SMiLe

The Rubber Duck Principle

Love You . . .
Love Life . . .

Good Rules for All

1. Be nice to one another
2. Think good thoughts
3. Try to do better
4. Say please & thank you
5. Smile
6. Be Happy with what you have
7. Listen to others
8. Be Helpful
9. Speak kindness
10. NEVER give up

EMBRACE WHAT MAKES YOU UNIQUE!

ke you your best friend

If caterpillars can CHANGE into butterflies . . . THINK what you can do!

Mirror, Mirror on the Wall

Clutter in Your Gutter?

For some reason, the 'stuff' we carry around in us—the negative thoughts—the anger and hurtful things we remember and re-live over and over—slow us down on our journey to Happy.

It's real simple: if you're full of Unhappy, it's impossible to fill yourself with Happy.

Start now. Stand in front on your mirror and have a full blown conversation. Just you and your mirror. Try saying things like "I'm willing to change." Is that little voice inside your head shouting back "No I'm not- I don't like change." For a change, let's not let the inner voice have the last word!

Think of it as a 'house cleaning'. Go through your head, your heart, your stomach, and see what's living there. Some of the things you find you'll love. So clean them up. Polish and shine them. Bring them out so you can use them more.

Then there are going to be things you don't need anymore. Don't want anymore. Things that don't belong in your life—just baggage you keep dragging around.

Now here's a trick that worked for me: when I first started doing this, I could not visualize it and just do it all in my mind. I needed to write it down. So I would take a cardboard box and a pad of paper and pen into the bathroom with me.

When a negative thought crossed my mind and made me feel 'ooky', I would write it down and put it in the box. I'm serious. I wrote down every negative thought, negative memory, negative idea I had that day. Then I would seal the box, walk to the curb and send it to the garbage dump with all the other trash I wanted to get rid of.

A few years ago I worked with a young woman who was seriously unhappy in her job—and other aspects of her life.

The Rubber Duck Principle

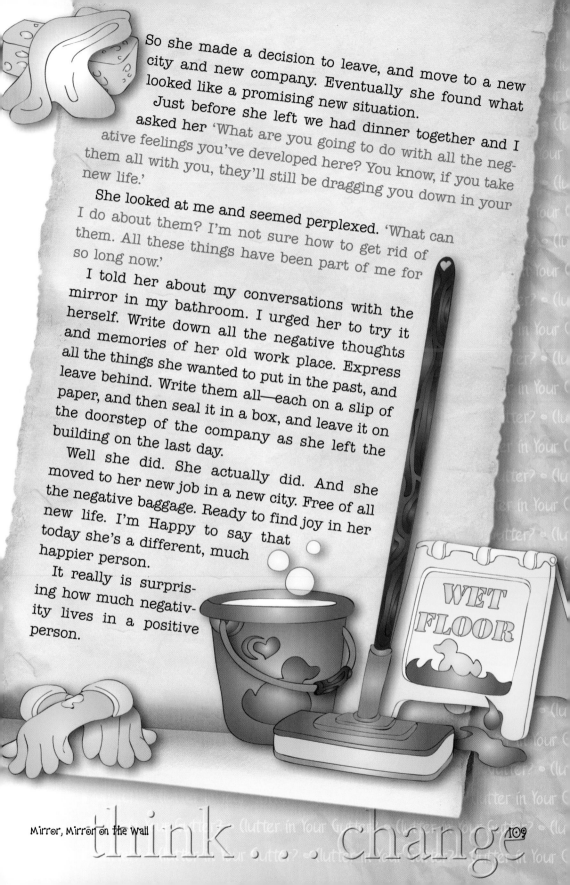

So she made a decision to leave, and move to a new city and new company. Eventually she found what looked like a promising new situation.

Just before she left we had dinner together and I asked her 'What are you going to do with all the negative feelings you've developed here? You know, if you take them all with you, they'll still be dragging you down in your new life.'

She looked at me and seemed perplexed. 'What can I do about them? I'm not sure how to get rid of them. All these things have been part of me for so long now.'

I told her about my conversations with the mirror in my bathroom. I urged her to try it herself. Write down all the negative thoughts and memories of her old work place. Express all the things she wanted to put in the past, and leave behind. Write them all—each on a slip of paper, and then seal it in a box, and leave it on the doorstep of the company as she left the building on the last day.

Well she did. She actually did. And she moved to her new job in a new city. Free of all the negative baggage. Ready to find joy in her new life. I'm Happy to say that today she's a different, much happier person.

It really is surprising how much negativity lives in a positive person.

Declutter Your Life

Our grandparents used to do Spring and Fall house cleaning. Days of hauling everything out on the front lawn, cleaning, beating rugs, putting out summer clothes, summer blankets, packing winter things away in moth balls till fall. Throwing things and giving away things along the way. In those days we didn't buy as much each year.

Declutter. If a room or closet needed painting, it was done at this time. Our grandma's did not work. Kids didn't have 45 after school activities. And each season had its job. Now, we work, we run, we stress. We buy more, we throw less, clothes don't have seasons. So our closets just begin to bulge and overflow. Unless we lose or gain weight, stuff just hangs in there forever.

Learn to let go of stuff. Help your children learn this lesson early in life. Let go of toys and every piece of artwork not necessary to save. If it doesn't serve your vision, let it go. Declutter your life, your mind, your heart.

Commit some time each day to purge. Keep a couple of garbage bags handy. If you purge a little every day, soon you have room in your life to bring in the new.

Build a clutter-free life.

The Rubber Duck Principle

This is...

the most powerful tool for change...

Believe you have already changed.
Pick an area where you think you've failed. What are your thoughts about it? Establish a new set of beliefs around it. If you think this won't work then it won't. Belief is an affirmation. If you think it will work, it will.

Can you Believe it?
You can't give 100% unless you believe. Prepare to win.

Take control of your thoughts.
Don't worry about how to do it. If you believe you can do it, the how to will follow. Now, act on it—Just Start.

Clear out the Clutter.
You cannot ever find peace if you are in a constant state of chaos and clutter.

But more importantly, you won't be able to have anything new in your life if you don't make room for it.

When the Inn is full—There is just no more room.
When you clean out the nooks and crannies you have made room for new people, new dreams to come in.

Let go of stuff.
It's just stuff. If it doesn't serve you, if you don't use it, it has to go.

My Wish for You

Some people are making such thorough plans for rainy days that they aren't enjoying today's sunshine.
—William Feather

Have fun being you. Sparkle...

Smiles when sadness fills you

Laughter with lots of friends

Courage to like yourself

Faith to believe in the real you

Sunshine after the rain

Angels to carry you by your bra straps

while you reach for your star!

What inspires you?

Like you...
Love you...

Be picky—be positive

I will say that it is a good idea to pick friends who have the same values as you do. If there ever comes a time in your life when you doubt yourself, you will want someone around who can help you remember the good things you saw inside of you once upon a time. And the only person who can do that is a person who shares your same values.

LOVE

Spend fun time with you!

Like you...
Love you...

"When you get right down to it,
the secret of having it all is loving it all."
—Dr. Joyce Brothers

The Rubber Duck Principle

Be friends with yourself . . .

Have an "ALL ABOUT ME" DAY!

It's 'all about me' Day

12 ways to de-stress

Breathe deep for 15 minutes

Go to bed early; sleep late

Find a quiet spot; for 15 minutes

Talk to no one; combine with breathing;

No tv, no radio, no music

Quiet

Drink Green Tea

Clear the Clutter from your house, your office, your car

Make room for new

Don't gossip . . . takes time . . . takes energy

It's negative; invest your time in the positive

Smile all day—no matter what!

Eat a breakfast—slow and enjoy it!

Have a day of giggles

Take time to enjoy what you have

Don't take yourself too seriously; laugh in the mirror

Have coffee with a friend

Do it all Guilt Free!

One Way I Changed My Thinking

All of you that know my story from my first book "PULL YOURSELF UP BY YOUR BRA STRAPS" know that I was living my dream life . . . I thought I had my whole world wrapped up in a perfect pink bow . . . I was living the dream of every young girl that grew up in the '40's and '50's . . . I had married prince charming . . . we had two children, a boy and a girl, we were well off financially, and were generally leading a rich and rewarding life. It was in a word . . . perfect.

Then on a beautiful spring day in 1981 it all ended in a split second. The love of my life dropped dead at my feet . . . and there I sat a poor widow with two children to raise and no knowledge on how to do it.

The three of us had some choices to make. We could lay down and die with him or we could work together to build a brand new life and make my husband and their father proud of us. We chose to move on with our lives and make a new one; a very different one from the one we had as a family of four. We worked, we struggled, we begged for help and we struggled some more.

I found that life is not a straight road that we are promised to travel down free and unharmed. I just wanted to get to where we were going. I was so tired of the bumpy roads, the detours, the dips, and the potholes. I wanted an understandable road map to follow to get my family and me back to living a dream life.

Then one day I just gave it up and put it in the hands of God and said, "Ok God, what do you have in mind for us? Just take us there. Show us the road to take on this journey." And he did. Our business finally began to grow and we were led to QVC and have become one of the most successful brands on the network with our Quacker Factory line of clothing.

THEN
ON A BEAUTIFUL
SPRING DAY IN 1981
IT ALL ENDED . . .

The Rubber Duck Principle

It has been a great ride. I have been living a new dream and have loved my new life. We have shined in our new business and our successes have been many. We just knew that this was it. I made myself at home and grew into our success.

For thirteen years life had been wonderful. There had been some rocks in the road or a flat tire every so often, but on the whole we were really enjoying our journey. I even began to think that maybe this was my destination. It seems that the more important your life is to you the more you want to keep it. I began to almost black out the bad things as they began to happen, to sort of stick my head in the sand. I became very comfortable and knew this would go on forever. I was finally secure. I didn't even notice there was a new wind a-blowin'.

CHANGE
HAPPENS

QVC had been sold to new owners and there were all new people hired for all the top level positions. All of these peo-ple were looking for new ideas and we were old ideas. We were not the new image. But I was stuck in my powerful human belief that nothing bad could happen to us. Nothing could happen to us. I deserved this life. We had worked long and hard to get here.

MOVE ON
QUICKLY

All of a sudden our journey was getting more complicated and challenging. Then the economy in this country began to go down hill and people began to loose faith in our brand. Great big gobs of my old friend fear began to seep into my great life . . . into my gut . . . and I became angry because of my fear. I began to rant and rave at the injustice of it all. How could this be happening to me again. I had said I would never loose my dream again. This just was not the life I had ordered. And the more I bitched the worse it got . . . the more I tried to fix it the worse it got. My son kept saying to me, "Mom we can't change this, we need to change the way we think about it." I would say why do we have to change . . . we're entitled to be successful and Happy . . . we were not causing the problems. Worry and frustration became my best friend, fear and anger my new neighbors. I liked my life just as it was. I'm comfortable, this is what I know, besides it's dangerous out there and I just might fail if I have to start all over again to fix

ALL OF A SUDDEN OUR
JOURNEY WAS GETTING
MORE COMPLICATED . . .

this. I started having trouble sleeping. I had no energy and became very irritable.

Then all hell really broke loose in my life. My best friend and partner of many years, Mary Ann, died too young of cancer and I lost one of my major supporters in this life. At the same time my baby brother was diagnosed with two brain tumors. I couldn't understand this either. How could it happen? We had never had any cancer in our family. Why is all of this happening in my life?

It didn't end there. My son Tim and his wife Karin lost her brother who was murdered. Karin's family and our's are very close and the pain of this was almost unbearable. Then my daughter who has had a heart condition all of her life almost died. I began facing depression for the first time in my life, but in the back of my mind I kept thinking if we just work harder and more we will find nothing has really changed. I really wanted to believe nothing had to change.

LIFE CHANGES. Change, change, change! I always say I really don't like change . . . but I don't know why I fight it . . . change happens whether I like it or not. Life changes and it's never the same again. This was beginning to look like one of those times. It's just how life works. We need to change our thinking or we get left behind. If we do not change, we will not be anymore. We will lose us. Fearful beliefs immobilize and can kill us. Remember life is a journey, it is not a destination . . . and we are always on the move.

My son Tim said that the first thought for me to change is my thoughts about change. He said let's believe change is really wonderful and will be great for us, it will take us to the next part of our heart's desire. We kept doing the same things over and over again and wondered why things didn't get better . . . it's almost funny . . . we are never going to get yesterday back. So lets embrace change.

So how do I go about changing my thinking about what is happening in my life? At this point I met a woman who shared a tradition with me from her life. She told me that in her world when she

The Rubber Duck Principle

wanted to make changes she would light seven day candles and ask God to move the people who do not believe in her on to bigger and better places . . . where they can live their heart's desire and to bring people into her world who see her value and see her vision. Well I lit my candles that day and they burned 24/7 in my office. They were a constant reminder to me to think new thoughts. And the negativity in my mind began to let go and I truly began again to trust God with what lay ahead . . . even though I didn't know what it was. I didn't know where we were going but I had decided I was going to enjoy the ride. When you let go of the fear and stop griping, you begin to feel good again and your Happy

Seven Day Candles

I have come to truly enjoy burning seven day candles and find that they are a constant reminder of the thoughts I am working on changing. I have found out that the colors of these candles are thought to represent certain concepts and I think it is fun to try and match up my thought changes to the color of the candle. It helps to really keep me focused.

Here's a few:
YELLOW—Creativity
GOLD—Money and prosperity
GREEN—Success and healing happiness
ROYAL BLUE—Laughter and joy
ORANGE—Self-confidence and career
RED—Health, passion, love
PURPLE—Wisdom
WHITE—Peace and protection
BLUE—Calmness, harmony, and peace

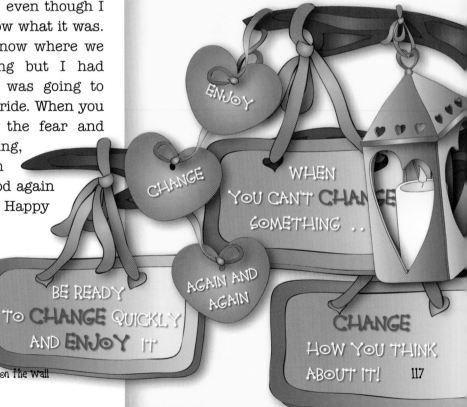

ENJOY

CHANGE

WHEN YOU CAN'T CHANGE SOMETHING . . .

BE READY TO CHANGE QUICKLY AND ENJOY IT

AGAIN AND AGAIN

CHANGE HOW YOU THINK ABOUT IT!

Life really is a fairy tale . . . it's just a new one every few years of your life . . . . .believe they do come true.

Remember go ahead and **CHANGE** her mind . . . . It's a woman's prerogative.

returns. Remember what you resists persists and grows larger. So the more you gripe about something, the more power you are giving it and just drawing more of the bad to yourself. Moving in a new direction frees us. I had almost forgotten how good it feels to succeed.

So start seeing yourself in your new life . . . see yourself enjoying your new success. The more clearly you can see it, the sooner it will come about. Make the dream big. Make it real and believable. Give yourself time to grow into it. Change leads to better if you just believe.

The quicker you let go of the old the sooner you allow the new to come into your life. When we are offered a new life sometimes we say "oh no, this is not what I do, I'm not trained for this, I want my old life back." Don't let fear stop you. A new dream is not as scary as we sometimes fear, just looking ahead can become exciting. Don't let yesterday fill up your today. New beliefs encourage new behaviors. When you change your thoughts, you change how you handle change. You can believe change will harm you and resist it or you can believe change is great and you will embrace it. It all depends on what you choose to believe. Change course. Acknowledge small changes as this helps you adapt to the bigger changes coming. Let the past go and adapt to the present . . . HOORAY FOR CHANGE . . .

hooray
for CHANGE!

The Rubber Duck Principle

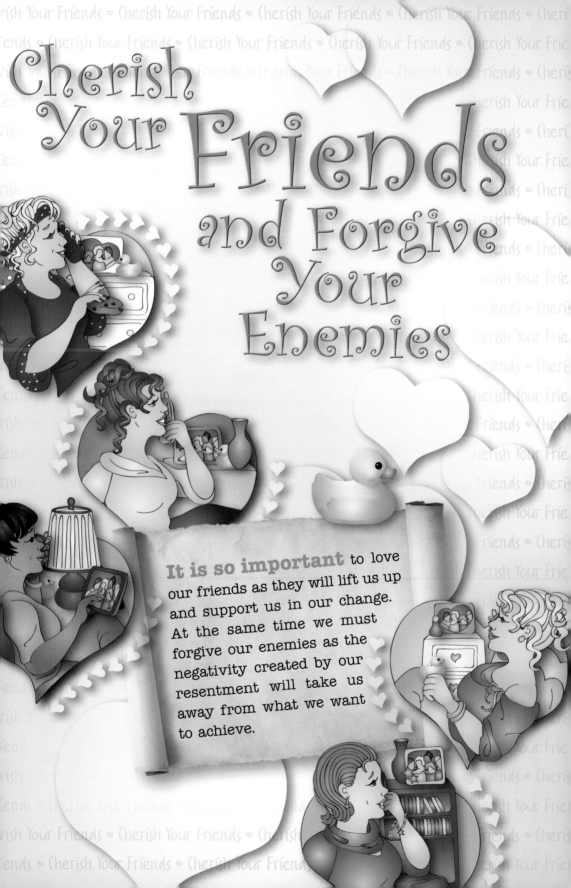

Cherish Your Friends and Forgive Your Enemies

It is so important to love our friends as they will lift us up and support us in our change. At the same time we must forgive our enemies as the negativity created by our resentment will take us away from what we want to achieve.

It Takes So Little To Be Special

When I first moved to Florida, flea markets became a fun day for me. Every Saturday morning off to my favorite one in Delray Beach we would go. One day we were walking around and ran into a women we knew from Green Lake, Wisconsin . . . Mary Wabiszewski.

We hugged, giggled and laughed! What were the odds of running into someone you knew like this? We shared stories of people we knew, what we liked at the flea market and how the kids were.

As I turned to leave, I commented on the flowers she was holding, "Oh, it's so nice you are treating yourself today to a pretty new bouquet." She said that they weren't for her; she had a couple of older women in her complex that didn't get out so she was bringing them flowers every Saturday. It brightened their week and she loved the short visit. It only took a minute, but it gave them a million minutes worth of joy.

I've had a wonderful, warm spot in my heart for Mary "Wabe" ever since. She is an angel on earth. This is what being a friend is all about.

close to your
HEART

WE

HUGGED

. . . GIGGLED AND LAUGHED!

Rubber Duck Principle

Take a moment to call an old friend

share your stories

This is what being a friend is all about.

A FRIEND IS LIKE A GOOD BRA . . .
HARD TO FIND,
SUPPORTIVE,
COMFORTABLE,
THERE TO LIFT YOU UP AND
IS ALWAYS CLOSE TO
YOUR HEART!

You are Wonderful

spread your JOY

brighten someone's DAY!

Million minutes worth of joy!

Cherish Your Friends and Forgive Your Enemies

Friendship

We don't need to walk alone . . .

When fear takes over . . .

call a friend!

If you can't BELIEVE in yourself . . .
find FRIENDS who
will support you & help you!

Just call on
"me"

"Whenever we **dream**
out loud, we're criticized
for being foolish by people
who really have no idea
how **special** we are."

**SOMETIMES
YOU JUST NEED
A FRIEND . . .**

Rubber Duck Principle

"Everyone needs someone to share their secrets with . . .
I'm so glad I have you!"

FRIENDS make you SMILE . . . no matter what YOU are doing

LIFE is a lot nicer when SHARED with a friend

Let your friends help with your dream . . .

dream

Always Remember
There is a new day every day—
There will always be someone there to help you
believe "today is a blessing"
There will always be someone there
to tell you "this day sucks"
The choice is yours . . .
Go Happy!
It's a good way to go . . .

Live It Fully
Cherish Your Friends and Forgive Your Enemies

When you're down & out

Call a Friend!

_____
_____
_____
_____
_____
_____
_____
_____
_____
_____
_____
_____
_____
_____
_____
_____
_____

Count friends as the blessing they are . . .

124

Rubber Duck Principle

. don't know
which way is
up . . .

_____

_____

_____

_____

_____

_____

_____

_____

_____

Friendship Warms the Heart!

Remember a time
when a friend poured out her
love and **warmed your heart.**

We shared smiles . . .
We wiped the tears
and through the years . . .
Our friendship has grown
along with us . . .
You are truly
a wonderful part of my life.

That was an OUTSTANDING magnificent, FABULOUS thing you DID

Good Friends . . . are always there.

Life is a Picnic

you make me smile

dream

Rubber Duck Principle

Girlfriends

Keep pictures of your friends around you. When you get to feeling a little low, just take a look. It will remind you of all the good times and giggles you have had with them and how they are always there for support. Friends always show up for surprise parties, send flowers for no reason, cry when you cry and laugh harder than you when you are Happy. They are so special!

Put friend's picture here.

Thanks guys . . . our friendship has carried me through lots of bad experiences and has made the good ones better.

You make me smile!

That's Life Enjoy it!

Little Acts of Kindness

Kindness Matters • Kindness Matters • Kindness Matters • Kindness Matters • Kindness Matters • Kindness Matters

Cherish Your Friends and Forgive Your Enemies

Bosom Buddies

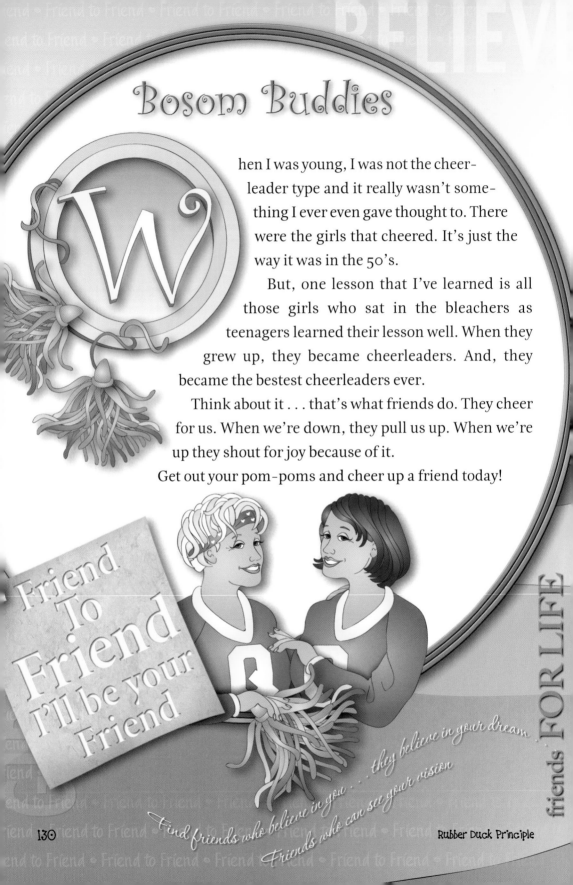

hen I was young, I was not the cheer-leader type and it really wasn't something I ever even gave thought to. There were the girls that cheered. It's just the way it was in the 50's.

But, one lesson that I've learned is all those girls who sat in the bleachers as teenagers learned their lesson well. When they grew up, they became cheerleaders. And, they became the bestest cheerleaders ever.

Think about it . . . that's what friends do. They cheer for us. When we're down, they pull us up. When we're up they shout for joy because of it.

Get out your pom-poms and cheer up a friend today!

Friend
To
Friend
I'll be your
Friend

Find friends who believe in you . . . they believe in your dream . . . Friends who can see your vision

friends FOR LIFE

Rubber Duck Principle

life has
it's MOMENTS...
...make them unforgettable

LIFE

Giggles
Giggles
Giggles

Simple Rules for Happiness
• Free your heart from hatred
• Free your mind from worries
• Smile more
• Expect more
• Believe more
• Know that a rubber ducky is unsinkable, and so are we!
• Believe in Magic!

Your Dreams

Worlds best shoppers

Believe

Every hug is a "Purr"-fect HUG

today...

...share your

VISION

Cherish Your Friends and Forgive Your Enemies

The Forgiveness Prayer

I've often told you about my dad and how he was my biggest supporter. But, as sweet as he was, my dad was the ultimate grudge holder. I think it was because of what we would call his German bull-headedness.

Like the time my mom and dad were at a friend Lenny's house for their regular Thursday afternoon game of Sheepshead (it's a German card game). Suddenly the host started shouting that my dad always seems to win, and it must be because my dad cheated somehow. Lenny continued to play, but finally got so mad that he stood up and stormed out of the house.

This wouldn't have been unusual . . . except for the fact that it was his own house he was storming out of!

Once he realized what he had done, the man came back in with his tail between his legs. My dad was very angry by this point about the accusation, but he agreed to complete the game. When that was done, my parents went home, and my dad refused to ever join the group for cards . . . and he never spoke to that guy again. Oh, how he would sputter about it to my mom every single day for the rest of his life. But he refused to ever do anything to make it better.

The apple doesn't fall far from the tree, and that is certainly the case with me. Unlike my dad, I could say that I forgave someone . . . but that was about as far as it went. My husband used to say to me, "Jeanne, you're a big forgiver,

Love Lifts When Life Hurts

but God knows you never forget, not one thing." And he was right.

Of course, I try so hard to hide anger. But that just makes it come out in silly ways . . . like when I talk to the steering wheel about my grudges. You can often find me pontificating and pounding away at the wheel while I sit in traffic, or a parking lot or my driveway. Yes, I have learned grudge holding from a pro.

The worst incident was when a young couple that worked for me started their own business on supplies they were stealing from our factory. I got so angry in my head that I started to think about having them put in jail . . . oops! The good girl had gone over the edge and become the nasty girl. I knew it had to stop.

So I started reading about forgiveness. What I came to discover was how powerful the anger and hatred of grudges could be. Not only could a grudge stop your life on a dime, but it could actually start you going backwards and losing what you worked so hard to get in your life. I could see that happening in my own world . . . I was hanging on to too much hatred.

There I sat and simmered, in between a rock and a hard place. I didn't just want to let those people off the hook for what they had done to me . . . it simply wasn't fair. On the other hand, I was tearing myself apart with every grudge I added to the list. It was time to pull myself up by the bra straps and put an end to the hatred.

That's when I asked for help, and

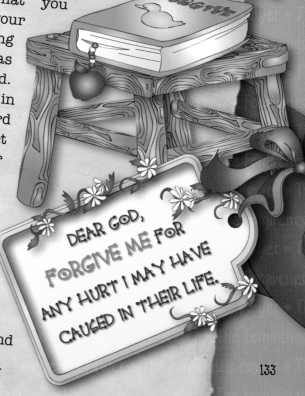

DEAR GOD, FORGIVE ME FOR ANY HURT I MAY HAVE CAUSED IN THEIR LIFE.

a dear friend told me to try saying a special prayer every time some of these bad thoughts would come into my head . . . and every time meant every time. Here's how the prayer goes:

Dear God, I ask (INSERT NAME) to forgive me for any hurt I may have caused in their life. And I forgive them for all the hurt they have caused in my life. I give this hurt and anger all over to you, I release it and I let it go.

It took a long time but I found it actually worked. The anger and hurt is finally gone from my life today. Now I just think of these people with wonder . . . wondering how their life has turned out.

I'll confess there are times a thought sneaks into my head like, "Oh I hope so-and-so got what they deserved." I'm very human, and this does happen. When it does, I clear that thought out as fast as possible and say my special prayer.

Dear God, I ask (him or her) to forgive me for any hurt I may have caused in their life. And I forgive them for all the hurt they have caused in my life. I give this hurt and anger all over to you, I release it and I let it go.

Of course there are many ways to say this prayer, so if you have another way to put it, or something you want to add . . . as long as it's positive . . . I say do it. The important part is that

I am always here for you . . . you are always in my heart!

LOVE

Rubber Duck Principle

you ask for forgiveness yourself and ask God to take the grudge you are giving Him so that you don't have to carry it anymore. Try it on ex-husbands, co-workers, mothers-in-law, old friends and even total strangers . . . you'll be surprised how well it works if you give it time.

The most important person to forgive? IT'S YOU!

Before we can forgive others, it's more important that we forgive ourselves. Even with ourselves we have to remember that the past is the past, we need to let any anger at ourselves go, and we have to forgive us so that we can pull ourselves up by the bra straps and move on. So this is what I often say to myself:

Dear God, I forgive Jeanne for all the mistakes she has made over the years, and I ask her to forgive me for any hurt I have created in her world. I give this hurt and anger all over to you, I release it and I let it go.

If you want to move on, I think you'll find saying this kind of a prayer for yourself is a very good place to start. Once you've forgiven, and forgotten, the road is much clearer, and you can move on toward your goal of finding your Happy!

I Love Love Love You!

THINK DEEPLY, SPEAK GENTLY, LOVE MUCH, LAUGH A LOT, WORK HARD, GIVE FREELY, TRUST GOD, AND BE KIND

"**RESENTMENT** is like drinking poison and then hoping it will kill your enemies."
—Nelson Mandela

"Take time for all things."
—Benjamin Franklin

The Forgiveness Box

Sometimes, people hurt us that have been a big part of our life, or we have big things to forgive people for, and it doesn't seem like a prayer alone can help. Well, I think it's still very important to say the forgiveness prayer we talked about, but there is another way I think can help you get rid of the big hurts.

Here's what you'll need to get started:

1 pad of paper

1 pen

1 small box

1 roll of tape

1 big dose of "me" time

1 open mind

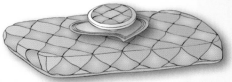

HELLO GORGEOUS!

OPEN MIND

All you have to do is sit down and write about all the things that are bugging you . . . little or big, it doesn't matter. Write down all the hurt you're feeling, and write down why you're hurt, or bothered, or just plain mad. Then put any paper you wrote on in the box, and tape up the box really tight, so no bad woo-woo gets out.

Then put the box out with the trash for the trash collector to take away. Say the forgiveness prayer again, and forget about the whole thing. Your big hurts, your big grudges, and all the little annoyances in between are on their way to the dump, where they belong. And you are out of the dumps, and back in a Happy place . . . exactly where you belong!

Adorabl
You!

The Time to Be Happy Is Now

Rubber Duck Principle

Happy's Gonna Happen Today (and Everyday!)

Let's continue to re-examine ourselves and our heart's desires even as we are having success at great new thoughts. This will keep us excited about the journey.

'Ole Road to Success

I'm a talker and I come from a whole line of talkers. My dad was the grand champion of talkers. As a child, I was embarrassed by it. He would talk to anyone and everyone, friends and strangers. It didn't matter to him; he just loved to chat with people.

I can remember going to Silver Springs Resort on our family vacation. We were just walking along when all of a sudden my dad shouts out, "Mayville. Mayville, Wisconsin." He directed it at a man in a wheelchair. Oh, my head whirled with embarrassment. However, the man seemed thrilled to see my dad, and as my dad chatted with him, they laughed and reminisced about old times and all the old business deals they had worked on. They had the best time! And, as they finished, the man thanked my dad and said he was Happy they had talked. He had been meaning to call him because he had a couple of deals that he wanted to share with my dad. 'Ole Ern's off-hand meeting and chatting had just brought in new real estate work for a couple of years.

When my dad started an auction, he never just got up and started selling like most auctioneers did. He would start by talking about the family whose farm he was selling. By the time he was done, you had grown to know and love this family and had felt the worth of their belongings. Then he would talk to the audience, acknowledge old friends, and tell a story or two about them. He would seek out the new people and find out why they came.

Rubber Duck Principle

He would always find a couple of people in the crowd who were experts in cows, farm equipment or the antique furnishings. Then, during the sale, he would call on them to back up the value of the piece. It brought a great deal of credibility to the sale and he brought about a very successful sale time and time again just by chatting. My dad truly loved people! It was a huge gift that he passed on to me!

I was born with a big mouth and my dad showed me how to use it. I became a chatterbox. Back when I was in business with my best friend, she would warn me over and over to keep my mouth shut. We would get on a plane and by the end of the trip; the whole plane knew everyone and their life stories. She really hated being in elevators with me. It was close quarters and the people had to talk to me! But, years of this chatting has given me knowledge about a lot of little stuff.

I've met a lot of fun people and they have given me a lot of joy. They have made me a more interesting person. So, how has all this helped me in business? First, I'm a story teller, and now I have great stories!

I've been kind to lots of people, and they, in turn, have helped me along the way. Don't ever think of it as idle chit chat. Caring about our fellow man is worth millions. Keep talking!

To look for the best is the way to get the best out of life and see the beautiful each day.

Beautiful

Enjoy

Joy Joy

Caring

Bubble Bath

Women's

Omen's hands . . . they cook and clean,
mend and fix, touch and soothe

Women's work . . . it raises
families, builds
businesses,
realizes goals and
is a winner.

But . . .it's our hearts that
make us special

Women's Hearts . . . we dream,
we believe, we survive

We care and it's full of gobs of love
for our family, friends . . . The World!

Give away your love
and watch it return
bigger and better each year.

We love you
and your gifts

You are special!

Happy Hearts

Hearts of a winner

Heart of a survivor

Heart full of love

Rubber Duck Principle

perfect for
play (everyday)

> Some
> people make
> the world
> special just
> by being
> in it.
> —Anonymous

take TIME TO play
make TIME TO play

Love and Respect Yourself

We just have to love ourselves! We have to love ourselves like we do our children and our spouses, and our friends. Go look in the mirror and say, "I love you very much, you are very special to me and you are very important in this

Reach for the Moon even if you miss, you'll fall among the stars

Rubber Duck Principle

world, and I believe in you with all my heart." And let's also respect ourselves like we have our parents and our teachers and our bosses. Don't let yourself or anyone else get in the way of taking care of you. Treat yourself like a very important person who deserves the respect of, and is, very valuable to everyone around you. Because you are, you absolutely are, the most important person in your world.

. . . FIGURE OUT WHAT YOU WANT JUST FOR YOU!

One really super good way to find your Happy and celebrate the spirit of childhood is to figure out what you want just for you. By focusing on you, you're allowing time to discover what God created you for, and you are the only one who can bring that discovery to life.

As you begin to take time for yourself, remember that you are born a magical being, and just because you may have lost some of the magic along the way does not mean it is gone forever. It's simply hidden deep down in your heart.

> "Magic is believing in yourself. If you can do that, you can make anything happen."
> —Johann Wolfgang on Goethe

Rubber Duck Principle

Happy is Success

Happy people are more
successful than unhappy people.

1st Step of getting more of what we want is to
Bless what we already have.

Whatever we concentrate on, whatever we think about,
We will get more of
This principle can work for us or against us

Focus on what we love
Focus on what we fear
Focus on what we hate
We will get more.

Every thought you think
Every word you utter
Every feeling you have,
Will automatically magnetize
more of the same.

Speak loving words—Attract Love
Speak Success—Attract Prosperity
Speak Healing—Heal the World!

Love You!

o, you look around you and you think, "I wish I were as pretty as she." Or, "I hope I can be as rich as he is someday." But a hard truth in life is that there will always be someone prettier, or someone richer, or skinnier, or smarter, or stronger, or younger. Someone who is more than what we are. That's it. That's a fact of life. You can't change it. And what have we learned to do when we can't change something? That's right, we change the way we think about it. The way to do that here is to start to love yourself more. There is an old saying that if a bunch of people gather around a table and everyone lays their troubles on it, you will always pick your own back up instead of choosing another. The meaning behind that is this: Maybe the gorgeous woman is suffering from a horrible disease. Maybe the rich man is desperately lonely and wants to end it all. So look to yourself and your circumstances, take a good long look, really think about it, and ask yourself, "Is my life so bad?" That is your first step on the road to loving you. Once you decide that things are not so bad, is it really that big a step to believing things are good? And once there, why not think things are GREAT. Let go of your jealousy and your envy of others. Remember those are two of the seven deadly sins! Who needs to look to others when you can look to yourselves and realize you have a beautiful heart, and you are rich in love.

it's good to be QUEEN

You are special!

Love who you are

"I am too Blessed to be Stressed and too Anointed, to be Disappointed!"

Queen for A Day!

Be blessed . . . pass it on

winners make things happen!

Happy's Gonna Happen Today (and Everyday!)

Think about it

The Joy Filling Station

When we're born I believe God fills our little bodies with JOY. 'May you ever be filled with the Spirit' is His command.

So where does all the JOY go?

I've given this a lot of thought, and I have decided I would stop worrying about where I lost it. And instead I would go about finding it. There must still be a little spark of that 'childlike Happy' in me somewhere, down deep, in the inner recesses of my body. (And in MY body, that's really deep!)

Did you ever go camping and build a bonfire? It gets to be a roaring fire; you sing songs, roast marshmallows, and tell stories. Then you go to bed.

The next morning the fire "looks" all burned out. Dead cold.

But is it? Deep inside that pile of ashes there is still some glowing embers waiting to be re-fueled if we only take the time to do it. In the case of the bonfire we must squat down and start blowing on it. Soon a little trail of smoke appears and then a tiny flame. Then we add a little kindling and finally some full size logs and within a few minutes the fire is blazing all over again.

I think our JOY is just like that. We can let it burn completely

All is wonderful. Sunny days ahead

c'mon, let's play!

FREE RUBBER DUCK WITH EVERY SMILE!

joy

out. Or we can decide to re-fuel it and get it burning bright again.

I believe that we all have a JOY tank inside us just like our cars have a gas tank. We all start with a full tank of JOY and as we travel on this journey of life we start using it up. Pretty soon we look at the gauge and it's getting very close to E-Empty. We didn't lose our JOY. We used it up.

It's a like a jar of Mayonnaise (which I love!). We use it to make a few sandwiches and a couple of egg salads and pretty soon it runs out. We didn't lose it. We just used it up.

Think about your bank account. You earn money, put it in the bank, and then you start spending. You know you can't keep doing it forever. You can't just deposit money once. You have to keep filling up your account before it runs out. We don't lose it. It gets used up.

It's the same with JOY.

We are full when we are born. We laugh. We giggle. We smile. We coo. We make happy. And loving parents fill us up with JOY every day and keep us happy.

But as we get older and take on the responsibilities of life we get so busy doing for others that we forget to watch our own JOY gauge and we let it run down. It seems unfair. But life doesn't come with instructions. We have to figure it out for ourselves. Just like with our cars we need to find a place to

Free Spirit Boost

FreeLIFT! with every SPIRIT BOOST

FREE RUBBER DUCK WITH EVERY SMILE!

SMILE

Make time to smell the Roses

Rubber Duck Principle

re-fuel. I like to think of this place as my "JOY Filling Station"

We ask ourselves 'How can I fill it up again?' 'Where do I go to find that little spark that's still burning inside?' 'Where is this JOY Filling Station?' (I used to think it was Baskin-Robbins but the fuel they sell doesn't last too long.)

For everyone "the station" is different. But we need to find out how we re-fill the tank or we'll run out of gas on the road to Happy and life will become dull and mundane.

Here again we need to get back to basics. Take time for ourselves and do the things that give us joy. Spend time with good friends and family. Play hooky from work and go play. Find the things that take stress out and put JOY in. Breathe deep. Read a good book. Go for a walk. This is how we fill the tank.

In life we don't get filled with JOY just once and live happily ever after. God expects us to fill it back up on a daily basis—by living a life that invites JOY.

GAS

WE HAVE JOY BY THE GALLON

"Start the buzz. Get excited."

big giggles

FREE!

FREE FILL UP!

re-fuel

Get Happy Music

Some of My Favorite Happy Music

1. Que Sera Sera—DORIS DAY
2. Catch a Falling Star—PERRY COMO
3. That's Amore—DEAN MARTIN
4. Everyday—BUDDY HOLLY
5. Top of the World—THE CARPENTERS
6. All I Have to Do is Dream—THE EVERLY BROTHERS
7. I Just Want to Dance with You—GEORGE STRAIT
8. Two Pina Coladas—GARTH BROOKS
9. What a Wonderful World—LOUIE ARMSTRONG
10. Today is the Day (Happy's Gonna Happen)
    —TIM BICE AND THE SPLASH

I LOVE Love, Love HAPPY MUSIC!

BE A STAR

List your **Happy music!**

1. _____
2. _____
3. _____
4. _____
5. _____
6. _____
7. _____
8. _____
9. _____
10. _____
    _____

Did you pick your happiest?

when the moon hits your eye like a . . . **big pizza pie** that's amoré

AMAZING things *sing along . . .* happen *when you*

Rubber Duck Principle

What ERA did you grow up with?

Was it Prince...so you love purple...

Was it ABBA? So you love mama mia you dance girl...

Happiest Picks

CHASE THOSE BLUES AWAY!

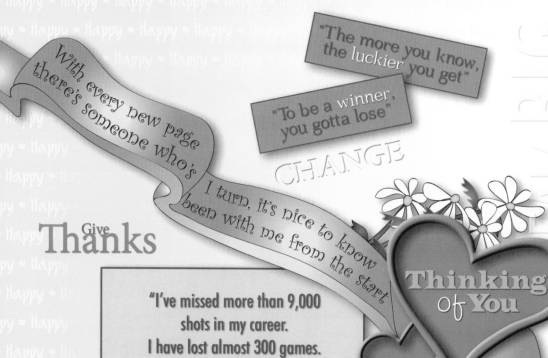

"The more you know, the luckier you get"

"To be a winner, you gotta lose"

CHANGE

DREAM BIG

With every new page there's someone who's I turn, it's nice to know been with me from the start

Give **Thanks**

Thinking Of You

"I've missed more than 9,000 shots in my career. I have lost almost 300 games. On 26 occasions I've been entrusted to take the game winning shot . . . and missed. And I have failed over and over and over again in my life. And that's why . . . I succeed."
—Michael Jordan

HOPE

STRENGTH

CHANGE

POSSIBILITIES ARE LIMITLESS

It's the time. It's the place. It Beckons . . .

Take Time to Play

With all the demands the world makes on us every day it is a challenge to stay on the road to Happy. It is important to take guilt-free time to really truly play. In our playtime remember also to make some pray time so we are constantly in touch with what is our Happy and the thoughts we want to have to stay there.

Always Play

You know as adults, I think we often lose our sense of magic and wonder sometimes. Despite the fact that there are new and exciting things going on in the world every single day, we tell our friends "same old, same old" when they ask us what the heck is going on in our lives. When is the last time you marveled at the world? When is the last time you were wowed and your chin dropped in amazement, and maybe you even drooled a little?

Or when is the last time you had a totally carefree day? A day where there was nothing to do, no responsibilities . . . I think that many of us have to go all the way back to when we were kids on summer vacation to remember that kind of day.

The problem with our busy lives is that we get too bogged down in the details. If we want to have a day off, we have to make all sorts of arrangements and plans. We have to figure out what we're going to do, and when we're going to do it. And we have to make a schedule for our day off. Then, of course we have to be back by such and such time in order to help out our spouse,

have a CAREFREE day

Take time to marvel at the world take TIME

The Rubber Duck Principle

REMEMBER

THE
RUBBER DUCK
PRINCIPLE

our family or our friends. The fact is that we are driven more by our "shoulds" and "oughts" than we are by our wants.

The worst part of it is that we believe with our heart and soul that "This is just the way life is."

Stop, it doesn't have to be this way!

believe with your heart and soul

"We don't stop
playing because we grow old;
we grow old
because we stop playing."

—George Bernard Shaw

celebrate the spirit
of childhood

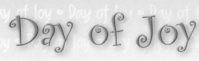

Day of Joy • Day of Joy • Day of Joy • Day of Joy • Day of Joy • Day of Joy • Day of Joy
Day of Joy • Day of Joy • Day of Joy • Day of Joy • Day of Joy • Day of Joy • Day of Joy
of Joy • Day of Joy • Day of Joy • Day of Joy • Day of Joy • Day of Joy • Day of Joy

Day of Joy

Love Yourself
Take time for yourself. Make space for joy.
Schedule playtime.

Here we are . . . Just hanging . . .

Think Happy Thoughts

HA! HA! HA!
HEE! HEE! HEE!

The Rubber Duck Principle

You brighten my day

You warm my heart

He will yet fill your mouth with laughter

You light up my life

Being Happy ...
Being Silly ...
Being Me!

LAUGHING

Let Go, Let GOD ...

" The more fun I have ... The more joy I let in ... The more sunshine I spread! "

JOY

JOY

SMILE

CHUCKLES

GIGGLING

My Dream Comes True ...
So Fast ...
So Easy

DREAMS COME TRUE!

I'm playing ... life is full of joy ...

Celebrate

Life can always use a little boost—so give a party.

There are a million good reasons to have a party. You can have a theme—it can be a big blowout New Year's Eve bash, or a few friends in for a cup of tea. It can be a lunch, brunch or dinner.

Keep a camera handy.

Crowd as many people as you can around the table—the more the merrier. The closer they are to each other, the friendlier they have to become. They have to talk to each other.

Use the kookiest, prettiest, funniest, most interesting or elegant cocktail glasses you can find.

Put a big punch bowl in the center of the living room floor with long, long straws. Everyone must lie on the floor together to drink. The trick at my age is getting back up! It's hard enough to do sober, but now when you factor in the tipsy, it just makes everybody giggle!

Candles, candles, candles everywhere. With candles, they know it's special.

Ask yourself—does it smell good, taste good, feel good, sound good and look good? Then it's a great party.

It's not what's on the plates that matter; it's who's in the chairs.

LIFE IS A PARTY . . . LET'S PLAY

TODAY'S the day to **CELEBRATE**

TIMES LIKE THESE
Time shouldn't pass. It should be stopped and captured and held on to.

kick back relax
Do a Little Hanky-Panky

TODAY IS THE DAY . . . HEY HEY

The Rubber Duck Principle

PARTY IDEA
"Let's Play Hooky Day"

- Invite girl friends to skip work and play hooky.
- Turn your van into a school bus.
- Make bag lunches.
- Milk & cookie treat as they get on the bus.
- Knee high socks and pleated skirts.
- School banners to wave.
- Hair in pony tales.
- School bag.
- Go to a flea market or a fall apple fair. Make it playful!
- Sing bus songs, play sign game and license plate game.
- No business talk.
- No cell phones—friends can answer, if it's not an emergency, the friend says, "Sorry, she skipped school today and is not around."
- Find a park for lunch.
- Play on the swings and teeter/totter.
- Slide down the slide.
- Play hop scotch.
- Give them yo-yos and hula hoops

Let your sweet, wonderful inner child come out in you. Buy tacky little gifts for everyone in your family.

CELEBRATE life's MEMORIES

SHARING the 'GOOD THINGS'

WHAT are you WAITING for?

DANCE yourself SILLY

Simple Joy JOY

invite a FRIEND

Live in the Now . . . Get Up & Go!

PUT ON YOUR BIG GIRL PANTIES AND JUST DEAL WITH IT!

Life's a Party Let's Celebrate!

Guess who's the guest of honor . . . YOU!

The time has come . . . let's get enchanted with life again. Let's forget the hurt and the worry and the voices who say we can't do this or that. Let's believe in the magic of life, the power of possibilities, and the wonder of the world around us.

The time has come . . . let's get serious about taking ourselves lightly. Let's ditch the frowns, the tears and those who won't laugh with us. Let's giggle like a child until it hurts, until we cry with joy, until we've got everyone laughing with us.

The time has come . . . let's learn how to play again. Let's put the work away, forget about the stuff we have to do and the people who tell us what to do. Let's buy ourselves a toy, and play dress up and invite everyone to come and play with us.

The time has come to LIVE our Happy! It's time to get out the ruts we all fall into from time to time, and
that you **CAN** play big . . .
that you **CAN** twinkle and shine . . .
that you **CAN** turn your dramas into dreams . . .
that you **CAN** bring magic, joy and wonder into your life . . .
    If you just believe . . . that you **CAN** do that, then you can live a life filled with sparkle. I know it for a fact, because I have lived it myself!

The Rubber Duck Principle

play again

Invite Everyone to Play Dress Up!

THE TIME HAS COME
TO LIVE OUR HAPPY!

SPARKLE

MAGIC

THE
time has
COME

PLAY
DRESS UP

LIVE
your
HAPPY!

TURN
YOUR
DRAMA
INTO
DREAMS

Believe

Lets Giggle Like a Child!

bring joy
and wonder

When Life Gives You Dandelions, Make Wine

If you can't change something . . . Change the way you think about it.
As a fun and simple example I submit to you "a common weed, the dandelion!" Most great lawn men work their heart out all summer long to create the perfect lawn. For some it is a ritual approaching a zen-like experience. And for most the biggest arch-enemy of the perfect lawn is "the dreaded dandelion."

. . . GOT A RECIPE FOR DANDELION WINE . . .

In Ripon we lived across the street from a park. It was a beautiful park, but the city did nothing about their dandelions. So when the wind blew from the south we would receive a brand new crop seeding themselves every few hours. One day my husband came in from doing a morning of yard work and asked me to come sit at the kitchen table with him. Our kitchen had a huge bay window that looked right out at the park. He said, "Jeanne just take a good look at the park and tell me what you see?" I sat there and thought, "Oh God this is a test. I hate games like this." But as I looked over at the park I saw a sea of yellow. It was beautiful and it was some of the first color of spring after a very long cold Wisconsin winter. They really were very bright and cheery and they made both of us smile.

He looked at me and said, "I have decided to stop

fighting with Mother Nature. I have decided to enjoy the dandelions, have fun with them, and go with their beauty." Then he said, "When they go to seed Jeanne what comes to your mind when you see those big white puffy seed balls?"

I smiled a huge smile and said, "Oh when we were kids we would pick them and have so much fun blowing the seed out into the world. Plus it was so much fun to rub the dandelions under our chins and see if we loved butter." We believed if your chin turned yellow you were indeed a butter lover. And then we would pick them and make necklaces and bracelets out of the stems and the flowers. Such great memories were wrapped up in these weeds.

My husband said he too had great memories of this maligned vegetation. His friend Danny Flanders' mom always made dandelion wine, and when they were in college she sent it to them as a treat.

We decided to make the dandelion our friend. I started picking the dandelions for fresh flowers on the kitchen table. Butch went and got a recipe for dandelion wine and we had a little winery in the basement. In the fall all of our friends were

If you can't change something change the way you think about it.

very impressed with his success in the wine business. We had a party and it did not cost us a dime to serve wine. We were having so much fun with the dandelions, and we were so proud of ourselves. All it took was changing our minds about the silly dandelion.

Then one day a fly dropped into the ointment. A dear friend named Roy Jackson who prided himself on a perfect lawn started to hassle Butch about the weeds in our yard. He was relentless, and it was getting to my husband.

One day he came into the house and said, "Maybe I should do something about these weeds." I reminded him of all the fun we were having with them, and not to get caught up in another man's stress mode over these little yellow flowers. Find another way to deal with this.

The next spring my husband is looking over the new seed catalogs and I hear him begin to chuckle and he shouts, "Jeanne, I have found a gift for Jackson." He ordered 6 packets of dandelion seeds and when they came he put them into a great planter box. He included fresh new potting soil, a bag of cow manure and instructions on how to make dandelion bracelets and necklaces for his wife and the recipe for dandelion wine. He wrapped this gift up in an article about the pleasures a dandelion can bring to this world.   Then he went over to his house late at night and left it on his front porch.

Well Roy was so busy trying to figure out who had sent the funny gift to him that he forgot to hassle us

I STARTED PICKING THE DANDELIONS FOR FRESH FLOWERS . . .

The Rubber Duck Principle

about our dandelions. Each year Butch would come up with a new gift to do with dandelions to put on Roy Jackson's front porch. Yes, he did figure out it was us, but it brought all of us so many laughs that the issue of it being a weed was long gone. Just look at all the fun we've had with our friends over the years by just one person changing his mind about something he had no control to change.

What is the dandelion in your life?

How to turn crappy into Happy

It's Your Time To Shine

Dandelion Wine

Dandelion wine does not require any special equipment to make. Just dandelions, some sugar and yeast, oranges, lemons and limes, and pots to boil water in. This recipe uses cloves and ginger which I think gives it a nice touch. If you have dandelions around, give it a try.

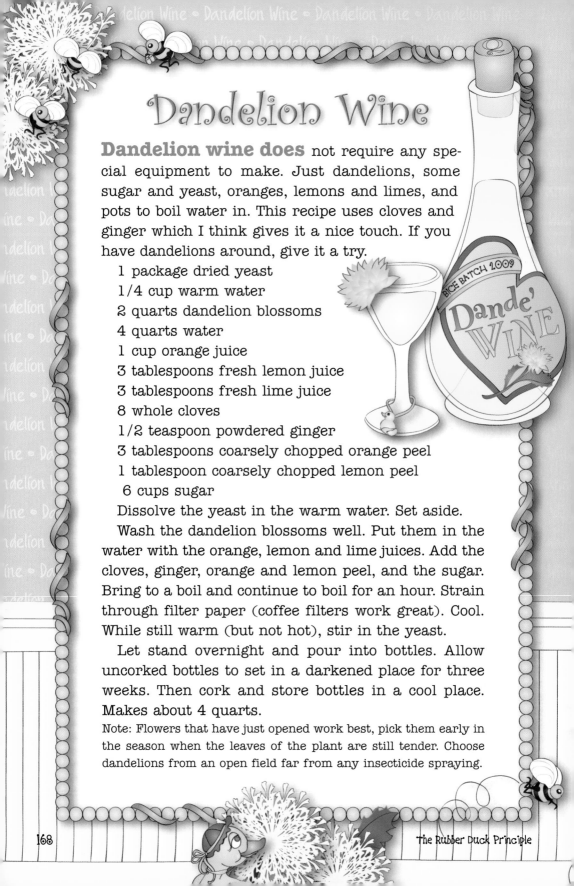

1 package dried yeast
1/4 cup warm water
2 quarts dandelion blossoms
4 quarts water
1 cup orange juice
3 tablespoons fresh lemon juice
3 tablespoons fresh lime juice
8 whole cloves
1/2 teaspoon powdered ginger
3 tablespoons coarsely chopped orange peel
1 tablespoon coarsely chopped lemon peel
6 cups sugar

Dissolve the yeast in the warm water. Set aside.

Wash the dandelion blossoms well. Put them in the water with the orange, lemon and lime juices. Add the cloves, ginger, orange and lemon peel, and the sugar. Bring to a boil and continue to boil for an hour. Strain through filter paper (coffee filters work great). Cool. While still warm (but not hot), stir in the yeast.

Let stand overnight and pour into bottles. Allow uncorked bottles to set in a darkened place for three weeks. Then cork and store bottles in a cool place. Makes about 4 quarts.

Note: Flowers that have just opened work best, pick them early in the season when the leaves of the plant are still tender. Choose dandelions from an open field far from any insecticide spraying.

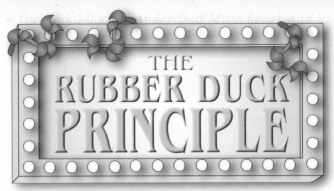

THE RUBBER DUCK PRINCIPLE

Stress Relief and Happy Enhancement Kit

he top-notch researchers that staff our high tech lab at Quacker Factory are involved in much more than the development of exciting new apparel for our loyal Quacker fans. We also have a whole team devoted to getting all of the stress out of life and putting as much Happy as possible into it. These scientists have chosen, as a model for this exciting project, the lowly Rubber Duck. The rubber duck has a distinct trait, which we humans would do well to emulate. No matter what happens to the rubber duck in his busy rubber duck life, he always floats calmly and unruffled in his pond just like he was created to do. No matter how hard the wind blows or how rough his seas become the rubber duck will not be sunk. Our research has shown that it is important to reach this same stress-free state where everything that needs to get done seems to happen by itself.

As a means to this end, our "Quack" scientists have developed a kit which will help to eliminate the stress from our lives so we can more effectively enjoy ourselves in all our pursuits, thereby adding more Happy. The elements that make up the kit are simple every day objects easily found in most local drug or discount

stores yet their combined effect on
our stress levels is profound.
They are as follows:

- rubber duck
- bottle of your favorite bubble bath
- toy crown or tiara
- something to use as your magic wand
- rubber duck beak with elastic band
- the child inside you

Use of the kit is simple. First, put on some relaxing
music and start a hot tub. Put in your bubble bath and float your
rubber duck in the warm and lathery water. And then put a duck
beak on your nose, a crown on your head, grab your magic wand
and climb on in. This will definitely put you in a "Quacky" state
of mind as you linger in a relaxing bubble bath and playing with
your friend, the rubber duck, from whom we've learned so much.

Additionally, when you go to your place of work, don't forget to
bring your duck beak, crown, and magic wand. You will find these
items to be indispensable as those around you try to put stress into
your life. There is absolutely no way anyone can mess with you
when you're wearing a crown and a duck beak and waving a magic
wand. This approach automatically guarantees a Happy and
stress-free encounter with anyone who comes your way.

This will definitely put you in a "Quacky" state of mind

Love yourself.

The Miracle of Happy!

I hope "The Rubber Duck Principle" has given you some food for thought (new thoughts of course). Remember that Happy is not a place where we will one day arrive. It is a daily journey. As we continue on this journey and have more Happy thoughts let's share these ideas with those around us, so not only will our lives be Happier but so will the people we encounter. Together we can change the world one Happy at a time.

Angels

Sometimes we feel that we are all alone, as life brings us challenges to overcome and hardships to bear. But when we least expect it, help can appear. It may be a kind word from a stranger or a phone call at just the right time, and suddenly we are surrounded with the loving grace of God. Miracles happen every day because angels are everywhere.

Miracles happen every day . . .

kind words

Bless

Believe in Miracles!

Let Yourself Shine

When we can see the joy in these perfect little bite-sized pieces of "good things," it gives you that funny feeling that the Lord is smiling on you and holding you so gently because you are someone Very special! And you really are Special!

angels are everywhe

Rubber Duck Principle

Angels ◦ Angels ◦ Angels ◦ Angels ◦ Angels ◦ Angels ◦ Angels ◦ Angels ◦ Angels ◦ Angels

My cup
runneth
over.

Psalm 23:15 KJV

Count Your Blessings Each Day!

There are Blessings everyday! Maybe little ones but they still count. Maybe it is a fresh pot of coffee you didn't have to make yourself . . . an unexpected phone call from an old friend. You got every green light on your trip downtown. The fact that you got in the fastest line at the grocery store. You found a radio station that played all songs you could sing along to. And, the parking angels sprinkled good luck on you with an open spot right in front of the store. Oh, my knees thank you . . .

Thank You
From the Bottom of my Heart!

Rubber Duck Principle

Wishing Works!

reach for the moon · light your dreams · bring your dreams to life · light your fire · believe · let your life speak · dream it · open up to possibilities · sparkle your dreams

Believe in Miracles!

always Believe!

You are a child of the universe,
no less than the trees and the stars,
you have a right to be here.
And whether or not it is clear to you,
no doubt the universe is unfolding as it should.
Therefore, be at peace with God.

—Max Ehrmann

Here are some ways to
CHANGE THE WAY YOU THINK . . .

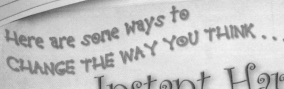

Instant Happys

Smile. Smile at your friends, your family and your neighbors. Smile at people you don't even know. Smile at the animals, the trees and the rest of the world around you. You can look up in the sky and smile at God.

Sing. Sing in the house, in the car and in the shower. Sing loud and out of tune. Fake the lyrics you don't know until you get to the lyrics you do. Sing like Rosemary Clooney, hold your invisible microphone, and look at your invisible audience, and bow deeply when they burst into applause.

Dance. Dance around the room, with a broomstick or a pillow, and hold it close for the slow songs. Sing along, and try out the move you'd never try in public. Make up the rest of the moves, and mess up the steps and buckle over in laughter when you do. Twirl a lot. Finish big, with something no one expected.

Avoid the news. This is a really important thing to do from time to time. If you've had a rough day at work, and turn on the news, you're usually more miserable than ever! Just switch the channel to a cartoon or a sitcom. Turn the page until you get to the crossword puzzle or your horoscope or the comics. Just because bad things happen in the world doesn't mean you have to know about every single one of them.

Giggle. Giggle, snort, snicker, chuckle. Laugh out loud; laugh so hard your lungs hurt. Maybe even pee in your pants a little! You start to cry you're so Happy.

Rubber Duck Principle

Say no. Let someone else take care of it for a change. Be nice, but firm, and do what's right for you, not what you've been expected to do. Have the respect for yourself to know when enough is enough.

Give back. Give a few dollars to charity or a few minutes to a friend who needs it. Give what you can, not what you're told to. Give because you want to, because you already have enough for yourself. Studies show that people who give little gifts to others are almost always happier than they are getting a gift.

Count your blessings. What's happened just today that you have to be grateful for? Who do you know that has helped you when you needed it? What do you do really well? Thank God for it all.

Learn something new. Read a book, take up a new hobby or join a club. Take a new road home or rediscover a road you haven't been down in years.

Watch a favorite movie. Maybe it's one that makes you laugh, or makes you cry (but only because it's THAT good). Or one that makes you remember the past, or forget where you are, or think about the possibilities.

It's a Wonderful Life!

Life is as EASY as you think it is!
Life is as HARD as you think it is!

think easy . . .

Big Time Long Term Happy Thinking

Accept that I deserve to be Happy. I am a good person, and there has been enough hurt in my life that it's time I balanced it out with lots of Happy. I love ME just as I am. Who knows what's coming tomorrow, so I'm just going to enjoy today. I have done the best that I could to get here. If I do anything better, it doesn't affect the gifted, talented, WONDERFUL person I am now. (This is the most important part of lifelong happiness!)

Be ready for more. There's nothing wrong with me. But I am ready for change. Ready for more. So I strive to become an even better me. That means I'm not trying to be like a supermodel, or movie star or other kind of mucky-muck. I'm not judging myself by anyone else's standards . . . I'm just trying to improve my life with what I already have inside of me. Because, I have everything I need to succeed already inside!

Embrace change. "I hate change!" How often does that come out of your mouth? People who fear change are unhappy people, so I am embracing change. I am forgetting my limitations and I am going to realize my full power and potential. I am going to stretch my greatness and my stardom and I am going to realize my goal. I will not accept anything less.

Be Happy with my unhappy days. Sure, I'm moving forward towards

I'M **NOT** JUDGING MYSELF BY ANYONE ELSE'S STANDARDS . . .

Dream Big

Rubber Duck Principle

reaching my goal of being Happy, but it's okay if I hit road bumps. I've learned my lessons, so I'm going to pick myself up one more time and do it again until I get it right. The important part isn't how I finish; it's that I started at all.

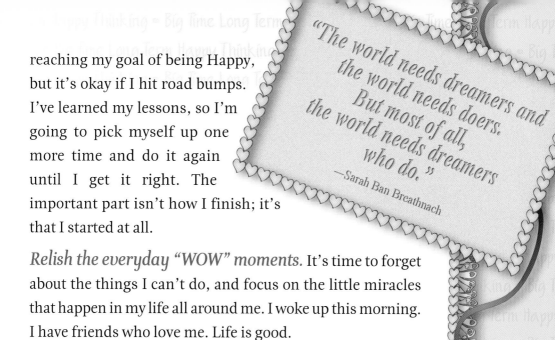

"The world needs dreamers and the world needs doers. But most of all, the world needs dreamers who do."

—Sarah Ban Breathnach

Relish the everyday "WOW" moments. It's time to forget about the things I can't do, and focus on the little miracles that happen in my life all around me. I woke up this morning. I have friends who love me. Life is good.

See the abundance around me. I have more than enough of everything in my life. God has given me the love, the strength, the will and the money I need to make my life what I want it to be, and I appreciate it all.

Be open to opportunity and the abundance I can't see. Good things are coming my way, and I'm ready for them. Whatever happens tomorrow and the next day and the day after that will make me stronger and more prepared to achieve greatness in my life.

Give Strength to Your God-inspired Dream

Dream a little dream with me . . .

Dream with your best friend . . .

Dream Big

I have just dropped into the very place I have been seeking, but in everything it exceeds all my dreams.

Let Your Creativity Sparkle

ur wings are fluttering with excitement. Optimism is one of the keys to living happily ever after. An optimist has an internal sense of power and strength. You can recognize that the situation can be dire. We need to solve our own problem. Stop being a victim; the process will enable us to grow as people. Spiritually, if we embrace the process instead of fighting against it, there will be a tremendous sense of satisfaction when it's all said and done.

We have become people who are addicted to being rescued. We have a tendency to avoid dealing with difficult situations, until it's too late and our only hope is to be rescued. Going through the angst while waiting to be rescued is a road block to living happily ever after. We deserve better, don't you think?

People are outraged by the sense of unfairness and betrayal. Have you ever wished you had your very own angel who would help you make your dreams come true? Wish no more, you are your own angel. Inspire, motivate, and move yourself. It's finally your time, your turn to go to the Ball. You've taken care of everyone else. Are you ready to make your own dreams come true? Thank you for dreaming back every time I dream.

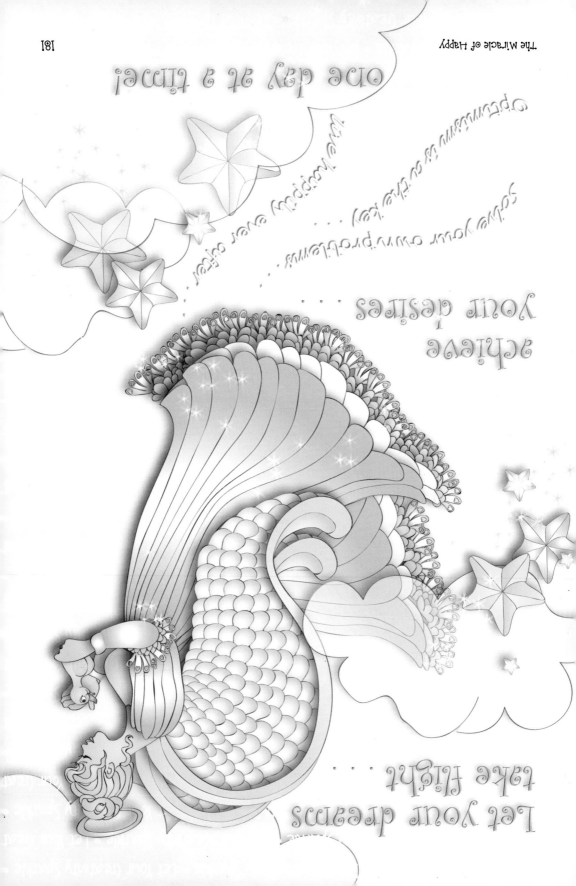

One day at a time!

optimism is a key...

we happily ever after...

solve your own problems

achieve your desires

Let your dreams take flight...

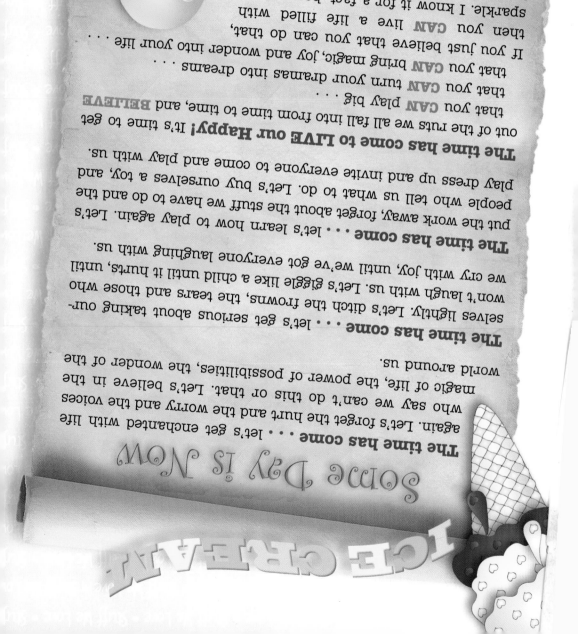

Some Day is Now

The time has come . . . let's get enchanted with life again. Let's forget the hurt and the worry and the voices who say we can't do this or that. Let's believe in the magic of life, the power of possibilities, the wonder of the world around us.

The time has come . . . let's get serious about taking our-selves lightly. Let's ditch the frowns, the tears and those who won't laugh with us. Let's giggle like a child until it hurts, until we cry with joy, until we've got everyone laughing with us.

The time has come . . . let's learn how to play again. Let's put the work away, forget about the stuff we have to do and the people who tell us what to do. Let's buy ourselves a toy, and play dress up and invite everyone to come and play with us.

The time has come to LIVE our Happy! It's time to get out of the ruts we all fall into from time to time, and **BELIEVE** that you CAN play big . . . that you CAN turn your dramas into dreams . . . that you CAN bring magic, joy and wonder into your life . . . If you just believe that you can do that, then you CAN live a life filled with sparkle. I know it for a fact, because I have lived it myself!

I Believe in You!

Joy!

About the Authors

I was born to be a pampered daughter, a well-to-do housewife, and a perfect mother. However God had another plan for me, and my journey in life. In 1980, my "1950's style idyllic" life changed forever. In one fell swoop my family went from very blessed and fulfilled, to filled with fear and at a loss for where to turn. My husband died and I had to figure out what life was all about. I did not like what I discovered. Life was hard and unhappy.

One day while sitting in a public bath playing with a little yellow rubber duck I finally got it. Life didn't have to be hard anymore. I finally understood that I could choose to be Happy. I thought, "Today is the Day!", and I found my Happy. I've gone from being the designer of Quacker Factory Happy clothes to a woman who wants to bring Happy to the world one Quack at a time. Come walk the journey with me. I want to show you that fairy tales do come true.

Jeanne—Creator of Quacker Factory

Lee Bice was raised a spoiled princess and still holds that favored position to this day. She studied at Parsons School of Design, but became a spoiled housewife instead of working. After the death of her husband she started working for her family, and you'll be Happy to know she is still spoiled. She now lives in Florida with her three dogs, Winslow, Dolly, and Gabby.

Tim Bice is a co-creator of Quacker Factory. His journey to success has been completed with the help of all kinds of friends and family. Enjoy what you read, his Mom speaks the truth. Tim lives in Delray Beach, Florida with his wife Karin and even more animals than his sister. He has a son James who lives in New York City.

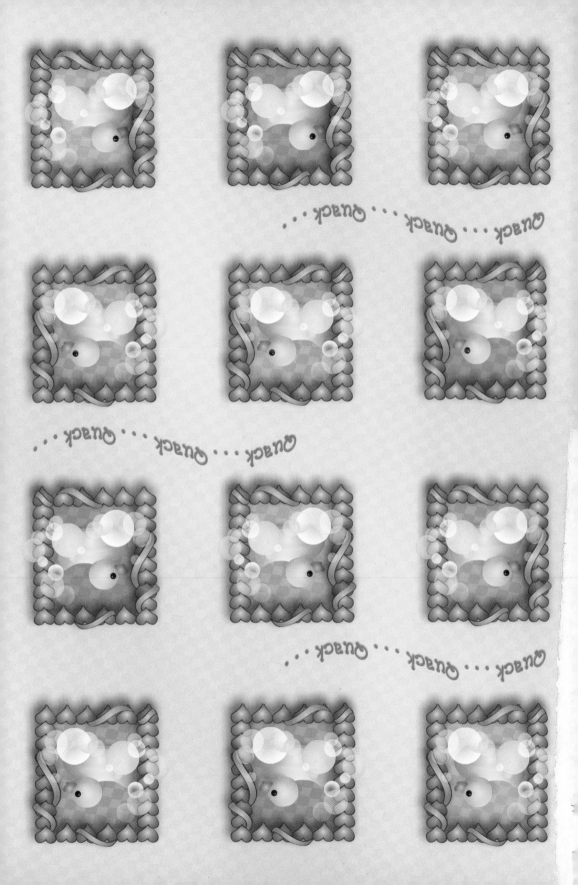

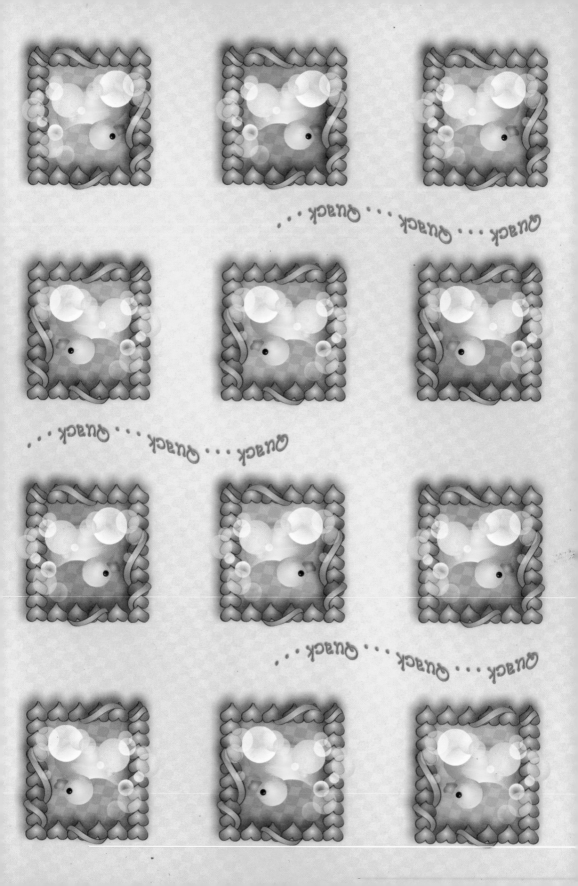